R.E.I. Editions

All our ebooks can be read on the following devices:

- Computer
- eReader
- iOS
- Android
- Blackberry
- Window
- Tablet
- Mobile phone

Brown Kittel

Lavochkin

LaGG-1 - LaGG-3 - La-5 - La-7 - La-9

ISBN: 9782372975353

Publication: February 2025

www.rei-editions.com

Translation from Italian to English by "R.D. Traductions"
www.rdtraductions.fr
r.d.traductions@outlook.fr

Brown Kittel

Lavochkin

LaGG-1 - LaGG-3 - La-5 - La-7 - La-9

REI Editions

Index

Lavochkin

The first Lavochkin fighter was designated I-22 and was also the first of the triad of new Soviet interceptors to take flight, exactly on March 30, 1939.
As will happen 2-3 years later with the Italian 'Series 5' fighters, and to tell the truth, as was already happening with the 'Series 0', the three competitors will all have a certain success and all will be rewarded with production contracts, but without for this reason resembling each other very much and even less being subject to the same evolution and operational success.

- Lavochkin, together with Gorbunov and Gudkov, had created a simple and robust fighter, relatively good-looking, but which had the problem of choosing strategic materials, or rather, the choice not to use them.

It was, in fact, the only one of the three that was built entirely of wood, except, obviously, for the fundamental elements such as the landing gear, the weapons, the engine, the ailerons (metallic and covered in fabric).
The retractable landing gear and M-105P engine were signs of relative modernity, and its maximum speed of 605 km/h was certainly noteworthy.

- The weapons were high-rate-of-fire, two ShKAS guns and one ShVAK gun.

Redesignated as I-301, it was later renamed LaGG-1, but for production it became LaGG-3.
The prototype proved capable of reaching 605 km/h, while the production model dropped (theoretically) to 575-580 km/h.
Despite its heavy structure, the real problem was the tendency to enter a spin in tight turns, which certainly did not encourage one to make the most of its already unexciting flight characteristics.

Furthermore , quality controls often made the expected flight characteristics uncertain.
However, it was successful as a tactical support fighter, especially used on the Finnish front, and within the limits of its autonomy, also valid for bomber escort.
It was capable of flying in harsh climates and often had skis, which, however, impaired its flight performance.

Lavochkin LaGG-1

The Lavochkin Gorbunov and Gudkov LaGG-1, also referred to simply as the Lavochkin LaGG-1 or by its prototype designation I-301, was a single-engine, low-wing fighter designed by OKB 301 under Semyon Alekseevič Lavochkin and developed in the Soviet Union in the late 1930s.

The first project of OKB 301, the LaGG-1 was not considered suitable for series production but formed the basis for the subsequent LaGG-3, the latter remaining operational in the VVS, the Soviet Union's Air Force, until the end of World War II.

- The VVS was the air force of the Soviet Union from 1918 to 1991 and an integral part of the Soviet Armed Forces.

It was dissolved in 1991 to be divided among the newly independent states.

Soviet political and economic trends were largely reflected in the domestic aircraft industry, which was responsible for supplying vast numbers of aircraft to the world's largest air force.

Aircraft used in the East were less flexible in roles than their Western counterparts.

Furthermore, the Soviet Union supplied all its allies, from the satellites of the "Warsaw Pact", to China, passing through the third world countries.

It should also be noted that the number of projects resulting in new prototypes was far superior to the Western one, as was the operational life of each individual aircraft, so much so that it was possible to find more than one model in service in the same role, as in the case of the MiG-17, MiG-19, MiG-21 and MiG-

23 simultaneously on the front line in 1976 and with comparable functions.
The discussions about the alleged superiority, or inferiority, of the Soviet machines have no foundation, since a direct comparison cannot simply be made: on the other hand, it was evident that every innovation beyond the Iron Curtain was initially overestimated, only to be criticized once it was put into service.
This was probably what happened at home too.
Another myth to be dispelled was the supposed speed with which the projects were developed, an illusion caused by the fact that the new devices were made public once the preliminary tests had been completed.
In any case, the Soviet designs were the result of remarkably original concepts (probably also because they were the result of original needs), but by the time they were introduced into service they had become obsolete, at least in some respects, compared to their Western counterparts.

- The Soviet Air Force was divided into five different commands, depending on the roles they had to perform.

The V-VS was approximately one million strong, and three million reservists, conscripted for 24 months, while the number of aircraft varied between 10,000 and 14,500.
To these were to be added another 350,000 men employed in strategic missile bases, several thousand SAMs (surface to air missiles, anti-aircraft batteries), tactical missile batteries, 70,000 naval aviation men and finally the coastal missile batteries.

The five autonomous commands were:

- National Air Defense.
  Numerically , it was the most important command of the air force, all surface-air units depended on it.

From early warning radar bases, to reconnaissance satellites, to anti-aircraft batteries, to ABM (anti-ballistic missile) batteries and finally to interceptor fighters.
Since 1948 this enormous complex of men and equipment has been placed under a single command, with headquarters in Moscow, and is under the orders not only of the Chief of Staff of the Air Force, but also of the Strategic Nuclear Self-Defense Force. The radar warning and control stations were positioned far inside the borders and were in constant contact with the operational units of all the Allied countries.

- Frontline Aviation or Front Aviation.
  It had at its disposal the largest number of airplanes, about 3,000, which were to provide air support for ground troops, interdiction of anti-aircraft fire and destruction of enemy aircraft.
  It was divided into 15 sub-commands, or air forces, as they were established in different, which in turn were divided into corps, usually three or four, made up of two or three divisions.
  Each division consisted of a certain number of units depending on the role: 40 fighters or 35 light bombers or 32 light transport aircraft or 36 medium transport aircraft or 30 reconnaissance aircraft or 36 helicopters.

- Strategic Aviation or Long-Range Aviation.
  It was the most offensive component of the Soviet Air Force.
  Directly under the command of the strategic nuclear forces it was divided into three sub-commands, two located near the Western front and the other towards the Eastern front.

It could count on approximately 900 units, the most famous of which were the Tu-95 Bear, armed with AS-3 Kangaroo, Myasischev M-4 Bison, Tupolev Tu-16 Badger, Tu-160 Blackjack, Tu-22 Blinder and Tu-22M Backfire.

- The Navy Aviation.
  It was under the command of the four fleets of the Northern Baltic, Black Sea, Far Eastern and Pacific and had approximately 75,000 men and approximately 12,000 aircraft.

- Logistics Aviation or Transport Aviation.
  It was primarily responsible for supporting strategic reserves and transporting troops, and had approximately 1,700 aircraft at its disposal.

The need for a new generation single-engine fighter pushed the Soviet authorities to issue a specification to be submitted to their own aeronautical design bureaus (OKB) relating to single-seater aircraft capable of a speed of the order of 600 km/h and powered by in-line engines of the order of 1,000 hp.
The power of the engines was no different from that of the radials of the previous generation of fighters, such as the Polikarpov I-16, but the better aerodynamic penetration, favoured by the possibility of creating a front part with a reduced frontal section and connected to the fuselage, guaranteed, potentially, at least in terms of horizontal speed and dive, definitely superior performance.
The various OKBs MiG, Yakovlev and Lavochkin presented their own prototypes, respectively the I-200 which later became the Mikoyan-Gurevich MiG-1, the Yakovlev Yak-1, built in mixed technique, that is with metal parts and wooden parts, while the one proposed by the latter, the Lavochkin LaGG-1,

was designed to be built entirely of wood, except for the components which could only be built in metal.

- Nearly all pre-war fighters were of mixed design: a compromise between the lack of duralumin and the cheapness and technological effectiveness of wood.

Metal allowed for enormous weight savings: with the same strength as wood, a duralumin structure weighed 40% less, but before the war a strategically correct decision was made, which oriented aircraft manufacturers towards a widespread use of wood in new aircraft.

- Thus, the possibility of mass production of aircraft by minimally skilled workers became evident.

Gorbunov and Lavochkin were the first to use wood in a fighter: their design is unprecedented in the history of fighter aircraft.

- Certainly this fact made it cheap and required very few strategic raw materials but, when the prototype was first taken to the skies, the pilots found it too slow in climbing and too heavy to control.

It is not appropriate to compare the all-wood English Mosquito with the LaGG.
The Mosquito was not designed for maneuverable aerial combat; its element was high-speed flight with smooth turns.
Well, as far as the wood used in construction is concerned, the Mosquito and the Soviet fighter are about as related as a hereditary nobleman from London and a simple peasant from the Tver province: one has exotic balsa wood, the other banal pine and birch.
Delta wood was used in the design of aircraft by Lavochkin, Gorbunov and Gudkov: it was used to make the longerons, ribs and some units of the front fuselage.

- Delta DSP-10 wood is obtained by hot pressing birch veneer impregnated with an alcoholic solution of phenol-formaldehyde resin, glued with VIAM-ZB glue.

Work began simultaneously on seven prototypes and a pre-series of 100 fighters was prepared.

Lavochkin LaGG-1 prototype

The first prototype flew on March 30, 1940, demonstrating inadequate range, ceiling, and maneuverability, and even potentially dangerous handling characteristics: although it was faster than the German fighter, as were all new Soviet aircraft, the defects were numerous and the technology used, with the exception of the armament, was judged not to be sufficiently advanced.

They therefore recommended various changes, also because in the meantime the "liaison dangereuse" between the Soviet Union and Germany had allowed access to several of the best German airplanes, noting how much more modern the latter were in structure and simpler in operation, starting with the Messerschmitt Bf 109.

The demands of the time did not allow for a fundamental redesign of the fighter, and the Lavochkin team therefore initiated a program aimed at alleviating the fighter's most serious defects: improvements were gradually introduced, while the design was subjected to a thorough weight analysis.

- The large-caliber machine guns were replaced by 7.62 mm ShKAS machine guns, and the 23 mm cannon gave way to a 20 mm one.

Various palliatives were applied for the maneuverability deficiencies and the first LaGG-1 prototype to introduce these modifications was designated I-301.
This also featured redesigned outer wing panels incorporating additional fuel tanks.
The I-301 had some shortcomings: heat in the cabin, poor visibility forward and sideways due to poor quality canopy glass, overheating of water and oil during altitude gain, insufficient longitudinal stability, extreme loads on the landing gear during take-off.

Technique

The LaGG-1 was a conventional-looking, compact, mostly wooden aircraft: a single-engine, low-wing monoplane with retractable landing gear.

The fuselage featured a single cockpit closed by a canopy connected to the back at the rear, a technical solution that did not allow for good rearward vision.

- The fuselage structure consisted of fifteen frames, four longerons and twelve stringers.

The keel was made integral with the fuselage.

The reinforced frames (no. 1 and 14) were made of Delta wood, while the longerons were made of pine beams of variable section: in addition to pine, lime and ash were also used in the fuselage structure.

- A metal support for the engine mount and weapons was fixed to the front of the fuselage.

All wooden parts of the fuselage were connected with VIAM-ZB glue, without the use of nails or screws.

The fuselage skin was glued with birch veneer: the thickness varied from 9.5 mm at the front of the fuselage to 3 mm at the tail.

The external surface finish of the fuselage involved gluing the veneer to fabric, filling and carefully sanding any rough areas before painting.

The fuselage was attached to the center section by four steel joints, while the wing planes were attached to the center section joints by bolts.

- The rear ended in a classic empennage with a single-fin vertical element and cantilevered horizontal planes.

The wing, like the centre section, was a two-spar structure, with the surfaces covered in plywood: the leading edge was glued with 3 mm thick veneer.
Wing mechanization included Friz-type ailerons with 100% weight compensation and four-section landing flaps, two sections under the center section, one under each deck, of the Schrenk type.

- The aileron and flap section frames were made of duralumin, the aileron covering was made of fabric and the flaps of duralumin, while a pitot tube was installed in the starboard wing console.

The wing, with a rectangular plan tapering towards the ends, was mounted low and cantilevered and incorporated, in the lower part, the landing gear mechanism.
The main landing gear with wheels retracted into the forward part of the center section.
For the wheels, special birch veneer domes were glued into the central section.

- The frame was retracted and unlocked by an air-oil accumulator and a hydraulic system.

The tail landing gear was retractable, while the landing gear wheels were equipped with pneumatic brakes.
This was a wide-track, front-wheel drive vehicle, retractable inwards and complemented at the rear by a support wheel positioned under the tail.

- Propulsion was entrusted to a Klimov M-105P engine, a liquid-cooled V12 capable of producing a power of 1,050 hp (772 kW), combined with a three-bladed VTSh-61P fixed-pitch propeller, later replaced by a three-bladed VISh-61 variable-pitch propeller.

The three-bladed, variable-pitch metal propeller VISH-61 with a diameter of 3 meters automatically maintained an engine speed set by the R-7 governor.
The propeller hub was covered by a spinner.
The engine frame, made of steel tubes, was fixed to the airframe at five points: the three lower ones, at the nodes of the front spar of the central section and the two upper ones, at the fuselage undercarriage.
The twelve-cylinder water-cooled M-105P engine was attached to the frame with twenty chromium-steel alloy bolts.

- The engine was fed by six carburetors, one carburetor for two cylinders.

Three fuel tanks are installed in the center section and another in each wing console: all tanks are connected in series via check valves to the center one, from which fuel is supplied to the carburetors via a fuel pump.
The central fuel tank has a capacity of 124 litres, the subsequent ones have a capacity of 114 litres and the wing tanks have a capacity of 98 litres, for a total of 548 litres: all tanks are made of AMCP aluminium alloy.
Oil is supplied to the engine via an oil pump from two tanks installed in the fuselage in front of the cockpit, with a total capacity of 47 litres.

- The M-105P engine is water-cooled, the capacity of the water system is 90 liters.

The radiator , honeycomb-shaped, was installed in a tunnel under the aircraft's fuselage: the water temperature was regulated by means of a special paddle, which changed the cross-section of the inlet opening of the water radiator tunnel.
The electricity source was a generator and a battery: the generator was located in the front of the engine frame, on the

right side, while the battery was located behind the armoured backrest of the driver's seat.

The fighter was equipped with oxygen equipment that provided the pilot with normal operating conditions at altitudes between 4,500 and 10,000 metres.

Technical Features

Dimensions and weights

Length: 8.81 meters
Wingspan: 9.80 meters
Height: 4.40 meters
Wing area: 17.62 m^2
Empty weight: 2,478 kg
Maximum take-off weight: 2,968 kg

Propulsion

Engine: one Klimov M-105P
Power: 1,050 hp (772 kW)

Performance

Maximum speed: 515 km/h at sea level - 605 km/h at altitude
Climb rate: 14.25 meters per second
Autonomy: 556 km
Tangency: 9,600 meters

Armament

Machine guns: 2 ShKAS caliber 7.62 mm + 2 Berezin UB caliber 12.7 mm, 220 rounds each
Guns: One Volkov-Yartsev VYa-23 23 mm caliber with 80 rounds

Lavochkin LaGG-3

The LaGG-3 was an improvement on the earlier LaGG-1, and was one of the most modern aircraft available to the Soviet Air Force at the time of the German invasion in 1941.

The Lavochkin LaGG-3 was a single-engine, low-wing fighter designed by OKB 301 under Semyon Alekseevič Lavochkin and developed in the Soviet Union in the 1940s.

The first OKB 301 project to reach mass production, the LaGG-3 was used in World War II by the VVS, the Soviet Union's air force, remaining operational, although progressively replaced by the newer Lavochkin La-5, until the end of the conflict.

- The LaGG-3 was essentially the production version of the LaGG-1, with a revised outer wing incorporating fuel tanks and armament consisting of a 20 mm cannon and two 7.62 mm machine guns.

Fixed wing slats were introduced, later replaced by automatic slats, and balance weights were added on the elevators and rudder, but were later discarded in favor of statically and dynamically balanced surfaces.

The weight was reduced as a result of a structural analysis.

- Deliveries of the LaGG-3 began in the spring of 1941, initially with the M-105P engine, but, from the end of the year, with the M-105PF engine providing 1,240 hp (900 kW) mated to a three-bladed variable-pitch metal propeller, increased fuel tank capacity and the installation of slats on the leading edge of the wings.

Later arrangements were made to replace one or both machine guns with 12.7 mm calibre weapons, the hub-mounted 20 mm cannon was replaced by a 23 mm calibre one and in some cases a pair of 12.7 mm machine guns were mounted under the wings.

- Three aircraft were each fitted with a 37 mm cannon and designated LaGG-3K-37, and one was powered by the 1,650 hp Klimov M-107A engine.

They were subjected to military tests in the 43rd Air Division and, according to the report, these planes managed to destroy five German tanks. The powerful armament literally pushed these aircraft to be used as attack aircraft: however, the new Shpitalny guns were still rudimentary and did not work reliably.
These three planes did not fight for long, as in mid-October they were shot down in the Vyazma area.

- Production of the LaGG-3 was completed by the end of the summer of 1942 with a total of 6,528 built.

Once in service with the units, the LaGG-3 was used extensively in the early stages of the war against the Germans, particularly on the Finnish front, and its performance proved satisfactory: however, the aircraft did not possess the characteristics of an interceptor that had been envisaged in the original design.

- It was, however, used successfully in bomber escort, ground attack and targeted strike duties, as a reconnaissance aircraft and as a bomber.

Furthermore, the LaGG-3 proved to be extremely versatile and reliable: its typical armament included a 20 mm cannon firing through the propeller hub and two 12.7 mm machine guns, while mounts for light bombs or rockets were provided under the wings.
By August 1942, a total of 6,528 LaGG-3s had rolled off the assembly lines, a remarkable number considering the aircraft's less than stellar performance.

The Lavochkin LaGG-3 on display at the Museum of the Great Patriotic War, Moscow.

- During the course of production, several further experimental prototypes were completed, built with the aim of improving the aircraft's characteristics.

Lavochkin, in particular, devoted himself to the task of perfecting it: after a series of failed attempts, success was achieved when a radically new engine became available.

- This was the Shvetsov M.82 radial engine which, once fitted to the LaGG-3, transformed it into a first-class aircraft, the LaGG-5 of 1942, one of the best Soviet fighters of the entire war.

Constructed primarily of wood, the LaGG-3 nevertheless proved surprisingly resistant to damage.

Although it did not work as well as other Russian designs, it represented a sort of stopgap solution until sufficient numbers of more capable fighters could be produced.
Further development of the aircraft included the addition of a radial engine which increased speed and performance: this prototype eventually led to the LaGG-5.

- The all-wooden wing, with plywood surfaces, was similar to that of the Yak-1.

The only difference was that the LaGG-3's wings were built in two sections.
Even with the lighter airframe and supercharged engine, the LaGG-3 was seriously underpowered, which led to many performance problems during combat.
The LaGG-3 was improved during production, resulting in 66 minor variants out of the 6,528 that were built.
Taking off with the LaGG-3 was simple if you followed these steps for a cold engine start:

- Open the throttle to approximately 15%.
- Set the mixture to fully rich.
- Close the water and oil radiator flaps.
- Set the idle speed.
- Power on: Default "E" key.
- Set the flaps to 20°.
- Wait until the oil cooler temperature reaches 40 °C and the water cooler temperature reaches 80°.
- Line up on the runway and lock the tail wheel by pulling back on the lever to hold it down.
- Fully open the radiator and oil cooler flaps.
- Accelerate at full power, maximum rpm. Correct the course with a small rudder input.
- As soon as you reach 140 km/h, center the lever and level out to increase speed a little.

- When reaching 190 km/h, rotate gently.
- Once in the air, pull up the cart and start climbing. Adjust the RPM and manifold pressure accordingly.

History

This aircraft set new standards in Soviet aircraft design, introducing a completely closed canopy and more aerodynamic lines, and was an unusual aircraft for its time: built almost entirely of wood, with the exception of the metal-structured moving surfaces, this fighter excellently combined the characteristic construction simplicity and lightness of wood with extraordinary structural robustness.

- Given the use of a material, wood, particularly abundant in Russian territories and given the simplicity of construction, the LaGG-3 was immediately put into production and at the time of the German invasion, several hundred examples were on the front line.

It can therefore be safely said that the burden of containing, in some way, the air supremacy of the Luftwaffe fell on the shoulders of the LaGG-3.

- From a qualitative point of view, the LaGG-3 was certainly not a champion.

Despite its good top speed and great range, the aircraft was really not very agile and was particularly difficult to fly, also due to the very poor visibility from the cockpit.
In addition to the static nature of the aircraft, its flight behaviour also posed problems: the airplane, in fact, had a dangerous tendency to go into a spin without warning during tight turns and had poor general stability, so much so that it represented a danger both for the enemy and for the pilots themselves.

- In any case, the urgent need for aircraft to be sent to the front pushed the Soviet authorities to give a high priority to the construction of the LaGG-3, so much so that within two years more than 6,000 units were produced, which equipped the combat squadrons practically until the end of hostilities, despite the entry into service of significantly superior aircraft.

Although the aircraft was not the fighter that had been hoped for and was clearly inferior to the German aircraft, its service was equally valuable for the VVS: in fact, given the great variety of drop weapons that it could carry and the possibility of adopting different calibres without particular difficulty, the LaGG-3 proved to be a versatile means for ground attack and assault, also ideal in the role of interceptor of enemy bombers.
From an operational point of view, the LaGG-3 was used intensively along the entire Russo-German front, but it was especially against Finland that the aircraft operated most with fighter squadrons, given, above all, the reaction of more affordable opposition and the presence of a fairly obsolete aircraft fleet, at least in the early stages of the conflict.
It is worth noting that three examples of the LaGG-3 were captured by Finnish troops, who evaluated and used them, while one example ended up in Japanese hands following the desertion of a Soviet pilot.

- This aircraft was tested by Japanese pilots, who also complained about its lack of agility.

The plan for 1941 called for the production of 2,960 LaGG-3 fighters: by 22 June 322 aircraft had been produced: the production rate was therefore well below the planned target.

- The target for 1 July 1941 was 805 LaGG-3s.

The project was not fully developed due to the extreme rush to launch the aircraft into production: in addition, Lavochkin had problems with the Gorky plant.

Lavochkin LaGG 3 model 29 prototype 01.

In fact, of the 100 people of the newly established design bureau from Khimki to Gorky, no more than thirty agreed to move: the remaining workers, and certainly not the worst, remained with Gudkov.

- With the start of series production, quality problems arose.

Complaints began to come from the units where the new fighters had been sent: the aircraft did not provide enough speed, the landing gear, given the weight of the two additional fuel tanks, tended to break, and there were failures of the armament and of the landing gear retraction and extension mechanisms.

Following modifications based on the results of prototype tests and the installation of additional equipment, the weight of the production LaGG-3s increased by 70 kg, the maximum flight speed dropped to 550–555 km/h, and the flight range decreased. During its use at field airfields, some serious defects of the aircraft came to light: suction of the landing flaps, very limited visibility to the rear, tendency to stall and enter a spin at low speed.

- In terms of weight efficiency and compactness of design, the LaGG-3 was significantly inferior to the Yak-1: the LaGG-3 design, with the same engine and almost identical armament, was, in fact, 300 kg heavier.

This was mainly due to the wooden structure of the fuselage, compared to the truss structure of the Yak-1; in addition, there was also a weight difference in the wings: the LaGG's console attachment points proved heavier than the Yak, which had no connectors.
However, the survivability of the LaGG-3, and especially its successor, the Lavochkin Lagg-5, was incredible.

- One of the first to receive the LaGG-3 was the 164th Fighter Aviation Regiment, stationed in the Caucasus.

In this regiment, Air Marshal N. M. Skomorokhov began his career as a military pilot and finished the war as a Major, having personally shot down 46 aircraft, eight of them in a group.
Three units of LaGG-3 of the 160th Regiment enabled GK Zhukov to escape to besieged Leningrad.
On the other flank of the huge front, the LaGG-3 series 1 were in service with the 44th Fighter Aviation Regiment of the Leningrad Front, transformed into the 11th Guards Regiment on 7 March 1942. In August 1941, pilots of the 17th Fighter Regiment used LaGG-3s to cover crossings of the Dnieper in the Kremenchug area.
In July, the 170th Fighter Aviation Regiment also received the LaGG-3, while in the autumn of 1941, the 69th Fighter Aviation Regiment was re-equipped with the LaGG-3 from the I-16.
One of the most successful fighter pilots of the Great Patriotic War, AV Alelyukhin, served in the Regiment: 40 victories achieved personally and 17 as a group.

- The LaGG-3 did not become the symbol of the battle for the skies of Moscow, but the regiments that fought on

LaGG-3s nevertheless made a significant contribution to the common cause.

On the Western Front, the LaGG-3 was widely used as a reconnaissance aircraft. By January 1942, the LaGG-3, together with the twin-engine Pe-2, was in service with the 3rd Reconnaissance Aviation Regiment.

In naval aviation, the LaGG-3s were used in the Baltic and Black Seas.

In the Baltic they served in the 3rd Regiment, the 1st Naval Aviation Regiment, awarded the rank of Guards on 18 January 1942 (previously 5th Fighter Aviation Regiment).

Technique

The Lavochkin LaGG-3 was a single-engine, low-wing monoplane, whose structure was, as mentioned, almost entirely made of wood: the main components were built using laminated wood panels, treated with Bakelite lacquer.
Only the control surfaces were metal with fabric covering.

- The landing gear was retractable, of the rear tricycle type, with a wide track.

The LaGG-3's wooden wings, with plywood surfaces, were trapezoidal in plan, with pronounced tapers at the tips: they were similar to those of the Yakovlev Yak-1, however, those of the Lavochkin were built in two sections.
The empennage was of the traditional type.
The fuselage was the same as the Mikoyan-Gurevich MiG-3 and, in the rear section, directly connected the cockpit to the fin, thus limiting the pilot's rear visibility.

- The Lavochkin LaGG-3 was powered by the Klimov M-105P, a supercharged V-12 engine producing approximately 1,240 hp (780 kW) and specially designed to allow the installation of a cannon between the cylinder banks.

The propeller was a three-bladed, metal type with variable pitch.
The LaGG-3 was armed with a 20 mm ShVAK cannon, firing through the propeller hub, and two 7.62 mm ShKAS machine guns, later replaced with two 12.7 mm Berezin UB machine guns.
The underwing hooks could accommodate bombs with a total weight of up to 200 kg or up to 8 RS-82 rockets.

- The LaGG-3 fighters of the first three series were virtually indistinguishable from each other.

Starting from the fourth series, the aircraft began to be equipped with more advanced Klimov M-105PA engines, with the same power as the M-105P, but equipped with an improved K-105PB carburetor.
The aircraft's fuselage also underwent structural changes: thanks to these innovations, the aircraft's take-off weight decreased compared to the first series and became equal to 3,280 kg.
However, during the serial production of the aircraft, there were manufacturing defects that seriously affected the flight characteristics of the aircraft: the flight speed decreased, 549 km/h against 575 for the first series, the rate of climb significantly worsened, 588 meters per minute against 735 for the first series, the flight range became equal to 870 kilometers, against 1,100 for the first series.

- Furthermore, the aircraft's handling had deteriorated.

In almost all respects, the aircraft was inferior to the German Bf 109F-4 fighter, delivered to the Eastern Front at the beginning of the war.
For this reason, the LaGG-3s always had a bad reputation: however, the aircraft did not deserve such an assessment at all.
Yes, it was heavy, slow in maneuvering, but in experienced hands it could easily compete with any enemy: on February 3, 1942, AA Gubanov on a LaGG-3 shot down three Bf 109s in one battle.
Another example, according to domestic accounts, on March 21, 1942, in the Rzhev region, five LaGG-3s clashed with 30 Luftwaffe aircraft, managing to shoot down five German aircraft without suffering any losses on their part.

- The next major change to the aircraft's design was made in the eighth production series.

Combat use of the LaGG-3 demonstrated the low effectiveness of the 7.62 mm ShVAK machine guns. Based on this, it was decided to remove both machine guns from the aircraft, leaving the ShVAK cannon and the 12.7 mm Berezin machine guns: this made the vehicle lighter and increased its maneuverability. Production of the eighth series of aircraft began in late 1941.

- Later, the eighth series was equipped with a 23 mm VYa-23 cannon, with a fire capacity of 370-500 rounds per minute and a muzzle velocity of 905 m/s.

This gun has proven its effectiveness against both lightly armored and unarmored enemy vehicles. A small number of aircraft of this series were equipped with an AFA-1 camera and were used as front-line reconnaissance aircraft.
The fighting in the early months of 1941 demonstrated the need to equip ourselves with fighters capable of being used as light attack aircraft to launch attacks in direct support of the advancing troops.

- The first modification of the LaGG-3 fighter in this role was the 11-series aircraft.

In fact, this series received, in addition to six RS-82 rocket launchers, also D3-40 bomb racks.
Thanks to these racks, the aircraft could carry light bombs weighing up to 50 kg: high-explosive FAB-50, fragmentation AO-25M and FAB-50M, or chemical KHAB-25 and AOX-15.
The aircraft were also equipped with VAP-6M (Aircraft Pour Device) chemical containers with 38 liters of phosphorus gas and an ASBR-2 sprayer capable of discharging all the gas in 3-4 seconds.
To destroy enemy forces, ZAP-6 incendiary containers were also used.

- The combat capabilities of the 11th series aircraft were further increased in early 1942, after the RO-82 launchers were replaced with RS-132 rocket launchers.

To make the fighter lighter, it was decided to reduce the fuel reserve, that is, to return to the original version of the LaGG, equipped with three tanks.

As a result, the 11 LaGG-3 series were not equipped with wing tanks, and, to compensate for the integrated ones, it was proposed to use underwing drop tanks with a capacity of up to 100 liters, which, however, were not widely used.

Attack versions of the LaGG-3 were used on the Kalinin Front in late 1941 and early 1942. The 129th Aviation Regiment, equipped with LaGG-3 Series 11 fighters, received the Guards rank for its victorious actions in early 1942: some aircraft of this regiment were converted to a winter version, replacing the wheeled chassis with skis.

- In 1942, production of the LaGG-3 fighter began in updated versions.

The first new variant was the 23rd production series, which differed from the previous ones by the larger turning stabilizer: all modernization works on the aircraft were aimed at improving the flight characteristics.

The next major innovation, designed to improve the aircraft's flying characteristics, was the replacement of the engine on the 28th series.

This option had been proposed by Gorbunov's design group: the LaGG-3 received a more powerful Klimov M-105PF engine.

Furthermore, by removing some weapons and equipment, the weight was further reduced, becoming 2,865 kg.

- Thanks to the reduction in weight and the use of a more powerful engine, the flight characteristics of the aircraft were improved.

The maximum speed of the LaGG-3 29 series was increased to 566 km/h and the rate of climb to 781 meters per minute.
The first aircraft of the 28th series was produced in June 1942.
Starting in August 1942, the RSI-4 Malyutka radio station was installed on aircraft of the 29th series. Also starting from the 29th series, LaGG-3 fighters were equipped with a VISh-150SV propeller with increased diameter.
The 33 series aircraft were virtually identical to the LaGG-3 29 series, with minor design changes in the fuselage and tail section of the aircraft.

- The most successful version of 1942 was the 35 series.

Numerous modifications were made to the aircraft to improve the aerodynamics of the fuselage: this made it possible to retain the good flight characteristics of the "light" version of the LaGG-3, while retaining all the combat capabilities of a front-line fighter.
The LaGG-3 35 series was produced at the GAZ-31 plant from August 1942 to spring 1943: a total of 2,771 LaGG-3 fighters were built in 1942.

- The most significant changes, however, were made to the LaGG-3, designed to destroy enemy tanks and armored vehicles: for this purpose, the design team led by Lavochkin undertook to modernize the fighter.

The first attempt to create an anti-tank aircraft was the LaGG-3 equipped with a 23 mm MP-6 cannon designed by Taubin: tests were carried out in early 1941, but, based on the tests, it was concluded that the 23 mm gun was insufficient to combat the new German tanks.

- It was therefore decided to build a version of the fighter equipped with a 37 mm cannon.

The idea of installing large-caliber guns on the LaGG-3 to combat enemy armored vehicles originated in 1940 by Gudkov, and the development of a fighter with 37 mm guns by Taubin and Shpitalny began after the government decree of March 1941.

The first gun was not attached to the M-105 engine and could not be installed in the LaGG-3, while the second, the Sh-37, was easier, but allowed only temporary mounting, as it was not designed for a large number of rounds: in fact, it was possible to load only 21 rounds into the aircraft instead of the required 50, and, even if the BS machine gun had been dismounted, the ammunition load would not have exceeded 30 rounds.

- The third LaGG-3, No. 23, built in February 1941, was converted into the first anti-tank aircraft.

To accommodate the Sh-37 cannon, the GS-10-350 electric generator was removed from the engine, and the lack of electrical power was compensated by installing an additional battery.

Additionally, both ShKAS were deleted and the BS machine gun mounting points were modified.

In place of the ShVAK cannon, the Sh-37 was mounted with 20 rounds of ammunition, with a spare magazine for another 2 rounds.

With an empty fighter weight of 2,511 kg and a full load of fuel and oil (402 kg), the aircraft's take-off weight was 3,318 kg.

In the rush to present the vehicle to the army, not all factory tests were carried out, as a result, the gun and its installation had to be modified at the Air Force Research Institute during state tests that began in the spring of 1941.

According to the test pilots, the fighter's piloting technique had not changed: when firing a large-caliber cannon, both single shots and bursts of up to 20 shells, the vehicle's flight mode did not change. The conclusion on the results of state tests, approved 16 days before the start of the war, stated: "After the improvements made, the 37 mm caliber aircraft motor gun of the VG Shpitalny system, mounted on the LaGG-3 M-105P, has passed state tests."

- In 1941, Plant No. 21 built the first 20 LaGG-3s with 37 mm Sh-37 guns (factory designation: Type 38), and the following year, before the plant switched to production of the LaGG-5, another 65 vehicles.

These aircraft became the basis of the 42nd Fighter Aviation Regiment of Lieutenant Colonel F. I. Shinkarenko, within which military trials began on the Bryansk front in March 1942. Initially, Gudkov, who had nothing to do with the artillery installation, was included in the NKAP commission, and only after the appeal of A. S. Yakovlev to the Air Force was Lavochkin appointed in his place.

Two squadrons (eight aircraft) of LaGG-3 shot down three enemy aircraft with cannon fire during an air battle: pilots who took part in this battle spoke enthusiastically about the cannon, whose shells left large holes in enemy aircraft and bomber fuselages.

- However, despite training, some pilots used up all their ammunition in the first attack.

It was also discovered that when firing long bursts of gunfire, the LaGG-3 lost speed.

The enemy, having learned about the appearance of such a powerful weapon at the front, literally began to hunt down the regiment: as a result, the tests had to be stopped, and the regiment was redeployed to the Moscow region, but not for long.

In May, the 42nd Fighter Aviation Regiment was sent to the Western Front, subordinate to Colonel B. I. Jansen's 202nd

Aviation Division: after almost every combat mission, the pilots reported downing enemy aircraft.
According to Shinkarenko, the squadron commander, Captain M. Gorbanev, was the first in the regiment to shoot down a He-111 long-range bomber, hitting it from a distance of 400 meters, almost double that practiced in combat for destroying air targets.

- In August 1942, 45 enemy aircraft were shot down in air battles using 37 mm guns.

In addition to the 42nd Fighter Regiment, the 188th Fighter Regiment of Lieutenant Colonel G.I. Cherepanov was also equipped with LaGG-3s equipped with a 37 mm cannon.
In August 1942, the anti-tank LaGG-3 with the M-105PF engine and a new VISh-61P propeller with a diameter of 3 meters entered state tests.
The aircraft had modified elevators and rudders with aerodynamic compensation, which reduced the load on the controls, and a fuel system with five tanks of the same volume; in addition, bomb racks were installed on the wings.

- In addition to the 37 mm Shpitalny cannon, there was a VS machine gun with 140 rounds.

In its conclusion, the Air Force Research Institute stated that the aircraft could be used to destroy tanks and armored vehicles with up to 40 mm of armor, as well as enemy personnel. But these conclusions had yet to be tested in combat.
Despite a favorable review by the main Air Force institute, the LaGG-3 with the Sh-37 cannon did not undergo further development.
Shortly thereafter, a 45 mm cannon was tested on the LaGG-3, made by replacing the barrel of the Sh-37.

The reason for the abandonment of the Sh-37 was the appearance of the NS-37 cannon, developed by AE Nudelman and AS Suranov in the OKB-16 in parallel with the Sh-37.
The history of this weapon begins during the life of the first head of OKB-16, Ya.G. Taubin.

- Unlike the Sh-37, the automatic operation of the NS-37 cannon was not based on gas extraction from the barrel bore, but on a drive by a moving barrel with a short stroke, with direct feeding via a cartridge belt: this circumstance subsequently determined its higher characteristics and reliability.

The most recent and advanced modification was the LaGG-3 66 series, which implemented the TsAGI recommendations in the field of airframe aerodynamics: based on the developments of the Yakovlev Design Bureau for the Yak-1B aircraft, some changes were made to the aircraft design.
The LaGG-3 featured a new canopy with 55 mm thick armored glass at the front and rear and a lowered fairing, which improved visibility to the rear.
Delta wood was gradually replaced by common pine, which had a significantly lower specific weight: measures were also introduced to reduce the take-off weight of the aircraft by lightening and modernizing the aircraft's equipment.

- In fact, the take-off weight of the LaGG-3 series 66 was reduced to 2,990 kg.

The flight characteristics of the LaGG-3 series 66, maximum speed of 591 km/h and rate of climb of 893 meters per minute, allowed it to fight on equal terms with the main German fighters of the Eastern Front, the Bf109G-6 and the Fw190A-3.

- However, the LaGG-3 was still inferior to them in terms of armament.

The aircraft of the 66th series were built in Tbilisi from the spring of 1943 to mid-1944: a total of 6,528 LaGG-3 fighters of the 66th series were produced.

By the end of the war, the LaGG-3 fought mainly in the Baltic and Karelian Isthmus, where the main enemy were the Finns, whose fighters were far from the most modern models. By May 1945, there were virtually no LaGG-3s left in combat units.

Technical features

Dimensions and weights

Length: 8.81 meters
Wingspan: 9.80 meters
Height: 2.54 meters
Wing area: 17.62 m^2
Empty weight: 2,680 kg
Maximum take-off weight: 3,346 kg

Propulsion

Engine: a Klimov M-105P, 12-cylinder V
Power: 1,240 hp (780 kW)

Performance

Maximum speed: 575 km/h
Climb rate: 12.25 meters per second
Autonomy: 1,100 km
Tangency: 9,500 meters

Armament

Machine guns: 2 ShKAS 7.62 mm caliber or 2 Berezin UB 12.7 mm caliber
Guns: one 20 mm ShVAK
Bombs: up to 200 kg in underwing hooks
Missiles: up to 8 (RS-82 or RS-132) as an alternative to bombs

Klimov M-105 engine

The Klimov M-105 was a liquid-cooled, V-12 aircraft engine. Developed from the earlier Klimov M-103, it was produced in the Soviet Union from 1939.
The M-105 was designed in the late 1930s using the experience gained with previous projects of the OKB led by Vladimir Yakovlevich Klimov: the M-100 and the M-103.
In particular, the M-105 maintained the same dimensions as the latter in terms of bore and stroke.

- The main innovations introduced with the M-105 consisted of the mechanical, two-speed supercharger, the double intake valve for each cylinder and the counter-balancing of the crankshaft.

Produced in approximately 129,000 units, Klimov's V12 acquired, during the war, the new designation VK-105, based on the system used by the Soviet authorities, which introduced the identification of the designer by indicating his initials.

Versions

- **M-105**

First version, produced from the end of 1939; it equipped some pre-war fighter aircraft and developed a power of 1,100 hp (820 kW).

- **M-105P**

First mass-produced version. The "P" designation indicated that the engine could house a cannon (in Russian, Puška) between the cylinder banks. It powered most of the Soviet fighters built before the war: power: 1,050 hp (780 kW).

- **M-105PA**

Improved version, produced from 1941: power equal to 1 200 hp (890 kW).

- **M-105PF (VK-105PF)**

Variant built starting from 1942: the modifications introduced allowed a significant increase in the power delivered, at the expense of performance at higher altitudes.
Despite Klimov's fears that the increased power could lead to a reduction in the engine's life cycle, the production of this version was approved at the urging of Yakovlev's top management, who equipped most of their fighters with this engine.
Power output: 1,260 hp (940 kW).

- **VK-105PF2 and PF3**

New versions featuring further increases in power output, 1,300 and 1,360 hp respectively, equal to 970 and 1,015 kW.

Klimov VK-105PF with a power of 1,260 hp (940 kW).

Note the 20 mm ŠVAK cannon positioned between the engine blocks which fired through the hollow propeller shaft.

- **M-105PD**

This version remained at the experimental stage. Specifically designed for use at higher altitudes, it was equipped with a two-speed "E-100" supercharger and developed a power of 1,170 hp (870 kW).

- **M-105R**

Version designed for use on bomber aircraft. Characterized by a decreased reduction ratio, it had a reduced transmission ratio, 0.59 instead of 0.666, and developed a power of 1,100 hp (820 kW).

- **M-105RA**

Update of the version specifically intended for bombers, also in this case, acting on the reduction ratio: power equal to 1,110 hp (830 kW).

Technical features

- Liquid-cooled 12-cylinder V-engine
- Powertrain: Carbureted, supercharged with a two-speed centrifugal supercharger (DCS) with gear ratios of 7.85 and 10, for increased power at low and medium altitudes.
- Displacement: 35.1 L. To reduce the load on the crankshaft main journals, counterweights were installed on the crankshaft.
- Bore: 148.0 mm
- Stroke: 170.0 mm

- Distribution: OHV, three valves per cylinder, two intake and one exhaust
- Fuel: 90-96 octane gasoline
- Power:
  - 1,050 hp (782 kW) at 2,700 rpm at 4,000 meters altitude
  - 1,100 hp (820 kW) at 2,700 rpm during take-off
- Specific power: 23.4 kW/L
- Length: 202.7 cm
- Width: 77.7 cm
- Height: 94.5 cm
- Compression ratio: 7.1
- Empty weight: 575 kg

ShVAK cannon

The ShVAK was a 20 mm caliber aircraft automatic cannon designed in the Soviet Union and used on VVS fighter aircraft during World War II.

- The 20 mm ShVAK automatic cannon was a large-caliber version of the 12.7 mm ShKAS machine gun.

The INZ-2 plant began production of 12.7 mm ShVak machine guns in 1935: in 1935-1936 the 12.7 mm ShKAS machine gun was rechambered for a 20 mm caliber and its serial production was launched.
A few months later, the 12.7mm version was withdrawn from production altogether.

- The automatic cannon version differed, therefore, only in caliber.

The 20 mm ShVAK cannon was produced in wing, turret and machine gun versions.
The machine gun version differed in increased length, the presence of a shock absorber and a number of other little things.
The ShVAK motorized gun, with some modifications, was installed on the T-60 and T-38 tanks in 1941-1942.
It was a gas-belt-fed, chain-disintegrating ammunition weapon, with cable or pneumatic loading for remote applications.

- Rate of fire: 700-800 rounds/min
- Initial velocity: 750-790 m/s
- Weight: 40 kg (88 lbs) without ammunition
- Length: 1,679 mm (66.1 inches)

The ShVAK ammunition consisted of a mix of incendiary, fragmentation and armor-piercing rounds.

In 1944 the ShVAK was supplanted by the 20 mm development of the 12.7 mm Berezin UB machine gun: the Berezin B-20 offered the same performance as the 20 mm ShVAK, but with the advantage of being significantly lighter.

Berezin machine gun

In 1937 ME Berezin began designing a high-power 12.7 mm synchronous air machine gun, firing a 12.7 mm infantry machine gun cartridge.
Between October and December 1938, the synchronous machine gun successfully passed factory and live fire tests, and on April 12, 1939, by decision of the Defense Committee, serial production of the 12.7 mm BS (Berezin Synchronous) machine gun was started.

- The machine gun's automatic system worked thanks to the energy of the gases released from the barrel.

The advantages of the Berezin machine gun included: the optimal arrangement of all automatic control units and separate gears, a high rate of fire, simple loading and unloading, and the simplicity of the gear device.

- Despite all the positive aspects, the BS machine gun also had some serious flaws.

The difficulty of reloading in the air with the aid of the cord system required great physical effort from the pilot, especially in the most decisive minutes of a battle.
Working on further refinement of the system, in order to eliminate these shortcomings and create a universal machine gun, Berezin developed the UB (Universal Berezin) universal machine gun in three versions, depending on the place of installation:

- Turret: weight 21.43 kg, with a rate of fire of 800-1050 rounds/minute.
- Wing: weight 21.14 kg, with a rate of fire of 800-1050 rounds/minute.

- Synchronous: weight 21.45 kg, with a rate of fire of 700-800 rounds/minute.

The basic details and gears of all three versions of the machine gun were therefore retained, with the exception of the trigger and the impact gears, which were subject to some modifications related to the specific nature of their use.
In the synchronous (UBS) and wing (UBK) versions, remote control was used via a recharging system in the event of air jams using compressed air.

- It was the first pneumatic machine gun reloading system to be installed on Soviet aircraft, greatly facilitating its use in battle conditions.

The ammunition load and ballistics were identical to those of the 12.7 mm ShVAK machine gun.
During testing, the UB machine gun operated without problems at an altitude of 9,000 meters at ±48 °C, continuing to fire with tight turns, combat turns, loops and dives.
From January 7 to February 22, 1941, the Berezin machine gun successfully passed service trials.
The 12.7 mm UB machine gun was ready in time for the war, which had been going on for two months and revealed the ineffectiveness of the 7.62 mm air machine guns when firing at air targets.
Production of UB machine guns was carried out at the Tula and Izhevsk factories.

- In 1941, 6,300 UB machine guns were built.
- In 1943, 43,690.
- In 1944, 38,340.
- In 1945, 42,952.

VYa-23 cannon

The Volkov-Yartsev VYa-23 was a 23 mm (0.91 in) automatic cannon, used on Soviet aircraft during World War II.
In 1940, Volkov and Yartsev created an automatic cannon, called TKB-201 for the new 23 mm projectile.

- The original intention was to create a gun capable of penetrating the armor of German tanks.

A total of 64,655 VYa-23s were built.
The VYa-23 was a belt-fed, gas-operated automatic cannon with a rate of fire of 600–650 rounds per minute, a high rate of fire for the caliber of the time.

- The gun was 2.14 meters long and weighed 68 kg.

Its main disadvantages were the powerful recoil and the very abrupt operation of the firing and reloading mechanisms, which reduced its service life and often caused jams that could not be repaired in the air.

- According to a US intelligence report, the VYa-23 used an enhanced version of the Berezin UB mechanism.

A new powerful 23×152 mm cartridge had been developed specifically for the VYa: the same calibre was later also used in the post-war ZU-23 towed and ZSU-23-4 self-propelled 23 mm anti-aircraft guns.
However, the ammunition for this later anti-aircraft gun had a different powder charge and primer and, therefore, was not interchangeable; in fact, the ammunition for the Volkov-Yartsev VYa-23 gun used brass cases and was not interchangeable with the steel-cased ammunition of the modern ZU-23 anti-aircraft

gun system. These two gun systems used different spacers and, therefore, required slightly different sized ammunition.
The ammunition was easily recognizable externally: while the VYa ammunition had brass cases, the post-war anti-aircraft ammunition had steel cases.
Ammunition for the VYa included incendiary fragmentation, incendiary fragmentation-tracer, and armor-piercing incendiary shells.
The total weight and fill of the HE shells were more than double that of the 20 mm ammunition used by the ShVAK and Berezin B-20 guns.

- The armor-piercing shell could penetrate 25 mm (1 inch) of armor at 400 meters (1,300 ft).

Despite the large projectile, the VYa-23 proved a disappointment in its intended anti-tank role.
German light tanks could only be destroyed if hit from the side or rear, while the front armour of all tanks was impenetrable.
Medium tanks could be destroyed if hit in the turret top or engine compartment from less than 400 metres (1,300 ft) in a dive greater than 40°, a very difficult manoeuvre even under the most ideal conditions, compounded by the difficulty of aiming at a small target.

RS-82 Missile

RS-82 and RS-132 were unguided solid-fuel missiles used by the Soviet Army during World War II.
Design work on the RS-82 and RS-132 missiles began in the late 1920s, at the Gas Dynamics Laboratory (GDL).

- The diameters of 82 mm (3.2 in) and 132 mm (5.2 in) were not chosen at random.

The fact is that the experiments were conducted with gunpowder projectiles with a diameter of 24 mm (0.94 in): their size is determined by the two main calibers of the rocket chambers, 82 mm and 132 mm, which were then stored for a long time.

- If 7 projectiles with a diameter of 24 mm are packed tightly into a cylindrical combustion chamber, the internal diameter of the latter will be 72 mm: the thickness of the walls of the chamber is 5 mm, so the diameter, or caliber of the projectile, will be 82 mm. Similarly, the caliber of the 132 mm missile appeared.

The first test launch of a solid-fuel rocket was carried out in March 1928, flying about 1,300 meters, and in 1932 successful test launches of RS-82 missiles into the air from a Tupolev I-4 aircraft armed with six launchers took place.
In 1933 GDL became part of the Reactive Scientific Research Institute, where it continued rocket development.
In 1937, aerodynamically efficient RO-82 rail launchers were designed to mount these weapons on aircraft.
The RS-82 officially entered service in 1937 and the RS-132 in 1938.

- The RS-82 missiles were carried by fighter aircraft, while the heavier RS-132 missiles could be carried by bombers.

The bomb body was propelled by the burning propellant at a speed of 340 metres per second, sufficient to sustain a flat trajectory for 1500 metres, after which it lost accuracy.

- Like most unguided missiles, the RS suffered from poor accuracy.

Naturally, the question of missile stabilization arose immediately. Many experiments were conducted to create turbojet missiles of caliber 82 mm and 132 mm, but the accuracy of the projectiles was unsatisfactory.
Moreover, with this stabilization method, about 28-30% of the weight of the missile charge was spent on the rotation of the projectile and, as a result, the forward speed and flight range decreased.

- It was therefore decided to switch to wing stabilization of the missiles without their rotation.

Initially, the 82 mm projectiles were tested with an annular stabilizer that did not exceed the dimensions of the projectile itself: however, shooting and blowing experiments in the wind tunnel showed that it was impossible to achieve stable flight with the help of an annular stabilizer.
It was therefore decided to use 82 mm missiles with a four-fin tail swing of 200, 180, 160, 140 and 120 mm.

- The result was quite clear: with a decrease in the winglets, the stability and precision of flight worsened.

In fact, during the experiments, it was discovered that with a 120 mm stabilizer, stable flight did not work: the projectiles stopped rotating immediately after the engine stopped working.

The use of fins larger than 200 mm proved too heavy, shifting the projectile's center of gravity rearward, which led to a deterioration in flight stability.

Eventually, the optimal dimensions of the stabilizers were found: a size of 200 mm for the 82 mm missiles and 300 mm for the 132 mm missiles.

- Initial tests showed that, when fired from 500 metres (1,640 ft), only 1.1% of the 186 RS-82s fired hit a single tank and 3.7% hit a column of tanks.
- The RS-132's accuracy was even worse, with no hits in 134 shots during a test.

Combat accuracy deteriorated further, as rockets were typically fired from even greater distances.

The RS-82 could destroy a tank with a direct hit, and the larger RS-132 could disable a tank even without hitting it directly, but by exploding in the immediate vicinity.

The best results were usually achieved by shooting at large ground targets.

Nearly all Soviet military aircraft of World War II were known to carry RS-82 and RS-132, often using field-made launchers.

A total of 12 million RS-type missiles were used by Soviet forces during World War II.

RS-82 Technical Features

- Length: 600mm (24 inches)
- Weight: 6.8 kg (15 lbs)
- Explosive weight: 0.45 kg (0.99 lbs)
- Fragmentation radius: 7 meters (23 feet)
- Maximum speed: 340 m/s (1,115 ft/s)

RS-132 Technical Features

- Length: 845 mm (33 inches)
- Weight: 23 kg (50 lbs)
- Explosive weight: 0.9 kg (2 lbs)
- Fragmentation radius: 10 meters (33 feet)
- Maximum speed: 350 m/s (1,150 ft/s)

Lavochkin La-5

The Lavochkin La-5 was a single-engine, low-wing fighter designed by OKB 301 under Semyon Alekseevič Lavochkin and developed in the Soviet Union in the early 1940s.
Initially designated as the Lavochkin Gorbunov LaG-5, it was an improved development, essentially based on re-engines, of the earlier LaGG-3.

- It was mainly used by the VVS in the final stages of the Second World War, becoming one of the most used fighters and remaining operational until the early 1950s.

After designing the LaGG-3, the designers split.
It soon became obvious that the only cure for the LaGG-3's shortcomings was a new, more powerful engine: the best alternative was the M-82 radial.

- Lavochkin managed to modify the LaGG-3 to accept this engine, despite the lack of official support, and the La-5 entered service in 1942.

The prototype conversion first flew in March 1942 with an M-82 14-cylinder twin-rod air-cooled radial engine, rated at 1,700 hp for take-off and the La-5 was cleared for service tests the following September with an armament of two 20 mm cannon.
With the completion of the conversion of the existing LaGG-3 airframes, minor modifications were introduced into the new production aircraft, the main one being the cutting of the aft fuselage deck and the introduction of a 360° vision canopy.
Thanks to its significantly superior power to the M-105P, the LaG-5 fighter acquired the qualities it had so lacked: its speed and rate of climb increased significantly, and its vertical maneuverability improved.

- Besides increasing reliability, the most important goal for improving the La-5 was weight reduction.

Replacing the electric starter of the engine with a compressed air one resulted in a saving of 20 kg, an improvement in the quality of the gluing by another 20 kg, the elimination of the weight in the tail by 15 kg, while the "cleaning" of the pipes and control cables led to a further reduction in weight.

- As a result, the take-off weight was reduced from 3,370 kg for the prototype to 3,200 kg for the production version.

Towards the end of 1942, the improved M-82F engine became available, producing 1,650 hp at 1,650 metres: aircraft equipped with this engine were designated La-5F and, from the beginning of 1943, the fuel tanks were revised.
From late March 1943, the fuel-injected M-82FN engine, which offered 1,850 hp at take-off, replaced the carbureted M-82F and with this powerplant the fighter became the La-5FN.
By the time the La-5 was withdrawn from production in late 1944, a total of 9,920 aircraft of this type had been built, including the La-5UTI two-seat trainers.

- In its developed version La-5FN was superior to German low and medium altitude fighters.

With the arrival of the La-5, and later the La-7, to front-line units, the era of the Bf-109's dominance on the Eastern Front was over: now and until the end of the war the “109” was outclassed, slower and more vulnerable than the air-cooled Lavochkin.

Lavochkin La-5.

- The FW-190, and its later modifications, such as the Ta-152, had a speed advantage above 4,000 meters, where, however, it could hardly find use on the Eastern Front.

In fact, most of the air activity there took place well below 5,000 meters, often almost close to the ground, and the record speed of those fighters could only be maintained for a very limited time.
At low altitudes it was not a great threat to the more agile Soviet fighters (just check the wing loading for the La-5 and La-7).
Its disadvantages included a cockpit equipment that was too simple, but quite sufficient for a day propeller fighter, a too short range, a bouncing-inducing landing gear and, in the early stages, very poor production quality.

History

After the LaGG-3, the first fighter model to be put into series production designed by his own design bureau (OKB), entered service revealing several shortcomings and proving to be inadequate for front-line needs, heavy to control (although better than the original LaGG-1, which actually did not even enter production) and slow to climb, Lavochkin was losing credibility with Stalin.

As his closest collaborator Semyon Mikhailovich Alekseev recounted years later, the party leadership had decided to favor the projects of Alexander Sergeevich Yakovlev who, with his OKB, had succeeded in supplying the VVS fighter units with the efficient Yakovlev Yak-7.

The need to counter the Luftwaffe's aircraft with an adequate number of fighters advised Stalin to increase production by starting a new line at Plant No. 21 in Nizhny Novgorod, which until then had been used to build the LaGG-3 as well as being the home of OKB 301 directed by Lavochkin, calling into question the future existence of the Design Bureau.

It was necessary to start the development of an evolution that would include the use of a more powerful engine, an attempt that had already begun at the beginning of 1941 with the new M-107 engine which, however, had not been followed up due to delays in the development of the new unit which was still too immature for series production.

The alternative solution consisted in adopting another engine unit with greater power, but availability had to be sought through an engine with a different architecture (the radial engine) as already tested in the case of the MiG-3 and the Yak-7 itself.

Lavochkin, however, was not, at least initially, convinced that the solution to the problem was to adopt an engine of this type, since those available at the time were poorly suited to the characteristics of the fuselage of his models, having a diameter that significantly exceeded the maximum dimensions of the V12 engine adopted up until then .

- Furthermore, the significant difference in weight between the two units would have compromised the overall balance of the model by dangerously shifting its centre of gravity.

Meanwhile, Mikhail Ivanovich Gudkov, who had collaborated on the development of the LaGG-1 and LaGG-3, had developed the Gudkov Gu-82 on his own initiative, a solution that combined the LaGG-3 airframe with the new 14-cylinder twin-star radial M-82, later renamed ASh-82.
First flown on 11 September 1941, it was able to express promising results, however, production never started due to a series of essentially logistical problems, including delays in authorizations which, according to some Soviet aviation scholars, were also attributable to political choices in the military hierarchy.

- In those circumstances, according to these sources, there were those who preferred to restore confidence in Lavochkin's group, preventing it from falling into disgrace in Stalin's eyes.

In any case, in the first months of 1942 the prototype of the new LaGG-3 M-82 was finally assembled and taken into flight, demonstrating that it possessed performances that were far superior to its predecessor, exceeding it in maximum speed by 40 km/h, making it faster than any aircraft in service with the VVS up to that point, thus justifying the immediate start of series production and also allowing us to glimpse further margins for improvement.
This first "stripped-down" version, being little more than a conversion from the LaGG-3, is also identified as the LaGG-5

or, given Gudkov's absence from the design team, more correctly the LaG-5.

Lavochkin La-5.

Production was decentralized to factories in Moscow and Yaroslavl Oblast: the results of these tests therefore induced the State Defense Committee to maintain Lavochkin's new aircraft in production at Plant No. 21, rather than converting it to the production of the Yak-7.

The first results of the operational use of the LaG-5 revealed, however, the presence of some critical issues in the aircraft: in order to obtain a further increase in performance, especially in terms of speed and handling, a series of tests were conducted at the TsAGI and TsIAM institutes, "Central Institute for the Development of Aviation Engines".

- These received four production examples of the La-5, which were subsequently subjected to aerodynamic modifications, including the modification of the upper part of the fuselage which allowed the use of a new, completely transparent drop-shaped canopy which, together with the use of a new version of the M-82F engine (the abbreviation F stood for "boosted"), gave rise to the La-5F version.

Other sources indicate that these modifications led to the aircraft taking on the definitive designation of La-5 for the first time.
The next development began in the spring of 1943 when, by coupling a further aerodynamically refined and structurally modified airframe with the use of various metal parts to an M-82FN engine (equipped with a mechanical injection fuel system), the La-5FN version saw the light of day, which remained in production beyond the end of the war, together with the more modern La-7.
Some developments of the La-5 did not see production follow-up: the use of an M-82 engine equipped with a Treskin TK-3 turbocharger was experimented, mounted on three airframes of the La-5F version: this modification, intended to improve the engine's performance at higher altitudes, highlighted problems due to the increase in weight which limited its performance.

- Also during 1943, the installation of the Shevtsov M-71 engine on the La-5 was extensively tested. It was supposed to develop 2,200 hp, compared to the 1,850 of the M-82FN, but the insufficient availability of these engines made it advisable not to undertake any modifications to the assembly lines of the La-5FN which had recently been started.

Unlike the previous ones , the training version called La-5UTI found widespread use. It was equipped with a second cockpit, intended for the instructor, mounted a reduced armament of a single cannon and lacked some on-board equipment, such as an armoured backrest, a radio and an oxygen system, in order to compensate for the increased weight it had suffered.

- Produced in over 10,000 units, the La-5 earned its designer the Stalin Prize.

Use

In its various versions, the La-5 was used mainly by the VVS: the only foreign armed force to use Lavochkin's single-engine aircraft was the newly reconstituted Czechoslovak Air Force. Poland also considered the possibility of introducing the La-5 into its forces in 1944 and several pilots received training from the Soviets between July 1944 and March 1945.

- The final decision, however, saw the Polish Air Force opt for the use of fighter aircraft produced by Yakovlev.

The La-5, due to its characteristics, was an aircraft to be used mainly at medium-low altitudes; in particular, below 4,500 metres, the performance of the La-5 was generally better than that of the Messerschmitt Bf 109 and the Focke-Wulf Fw 190A. The first examples of the LaG-5 were delivered in the spring of 1942 to the units engaged on the Finnish front: these were machines intended mainly for an initial operational evaluation of the model.
The pilots, who until then had used the I-16, the MiG-3 and the LaGG-3, had no particular difficulty in getting used to the new aircraft, while particular appreciation came from the departments that took care of the maintenance of the aircraft: the greater simplicity of the air-cooled engine and the ability of the aircraft to absorb the blows of the adversaries were considered a considerable quality, in order to keep the machines constantly operational in the harsh Finnish climate and on a vast front that was difficult to supply with spare parts and consumables.
The successes achieved against Finnish aircraft, which fielded the Fokker D.XXI, the Morane-Saulnier MS.406 and the Brewster F2A Buffalo, meant that the La-5 replaced all

remaining Soviet aircraft on the northern front, with the exception of the Yakovlev Yak-1.

- The first large-scale use of the La-5 took place in the winter of 1942 during the Battle of Stalingrad, followed shortly after by the La-5F series aircraft.

The following year, during the Battle of Kursk, the units received aircraft of the La-5FN version.
The tasks for which the La-5s were assigned were varied and ranged from escorting bombers to ground attack missions in which, often armed with bombs and shaped-charge rockets, the Lavochkins supported the Ilyushin Il-2 Šturmoviks, subsequently providing them with cover against possible enemy attacks.

- Among the pilots who boasted the greatest successes with the La-5 were several aviation aces, including Ivan Nikitovič Kozhedub and Alexander Ivanovich Pokryškin, who were awarded the title of Hero of the Soviet Union three times, and Kirill Alekseevič Evstigneev who achieved 52 kills while flying Lavochkin's fighters.

The revived Czechoslovak Air Force, operating under Soviet command, received Lavochin La-5FNs which were assigned to the 1st Mixed Air Division, formed in the Soviet Union on 1 June 1944.

- This unit also included 20 pilots who had previously been members of the Czechoslovak Squadrons of the Royal Air Force (Nos. 310, 312, 313), including Colonel František Fajtl.

The 1st Mixed Air Division was able to "return" to Prague on 15 May 1945 and subsequently the units equipped with Lavochkin were deployed to Slovakia.

After the war, the aircraft were grounded as they were considered to be subject to severe deterioration if left outside the hangars for a long time: an investigation by the Czechoslovak authorities, however, dispelled any doubts and the Lavochkins were once again brought back into operational service.

Technique

The La-5 was a single-engine, wooden, low-wing aircraft: as with the LaGG-3, the main structural material of the airframe was pine, while Delta wood was used to make the wing spars and some frames.

The wooden parts of the aircraft were glued together using VIAM-B-3 resin glue or KM-1 urea glue.

- The wing, assembled from NACA-23016 and NACA-23010 profiles, was technologically divided into a central section and two two-spar consoles with plywood working skins.

The wings were made entirely of wood, with only the control surfaces made of metal and covered in fabric: in particular, in addition to the ailerons located in the external area of the wing panels, there were hyperlifts on the leading edge of the wing.

The empennage was of the classic type, with the elevators placed at the base of the fin.

Plywood boxes for the fuel tanks were glued between the spars of the centre section, while the nose section contained domes for the landing gear wheels.

- The spars were made of wood with delta wooden shelves: on the La-5FN Type 41 fighters of Plant No. 21, starting in 1944, metal spars were installed.

The Schrenk-type flaps and Frize-type ailerons with duralumin frames, covered with percale, were fixed to the consoles with plywood covering.

- There was a trim on the left aileron.

The trim acts as a regulator of the control surfaces.

Its position on board an aircraft is not fixed, but can vary depending on the reference model: for example, the trim of an airplane can be fixed to the elevator, the ailerons or the rudder.
This instrument determines, in fact, the maintenance of the aircraft in the correct direction and attitude during the flight.
The term "trim" refers to the trim tabs, small mobile wings usually located on the elevator and, more rarely, on the rudder of aircraft.

- Generally speaking, it can be said that it is found on surfaces that have the function of lowering or raising the aircraft.

To make these movements happen, pilots must push the stick forward to make the aircraft descend, or pull it towards themselves to gain altitude. The Trims, in this case, come to the aid of the pilot, who will not have to continually leverage the stick to overcome the aerodynamic forces acting on the aircraft.

- Consequently, the function of the aircraft trim is to lighten the controls, until they stabilize.

This is because the instrument cancels the force that the pilot applies to the elevator, so that he can release the control stick, which will remain in the desired position.
The fuselage consisted of a metal front truss and a wooden monocoque, made in a single piece with the keel.
Its structure consisted of four stringers and 15 frames.
The fuselage was firmly attached to the center section by four steel joints.

- The cockpit was enclosed by a sliding canopy, which locked in the open and closed positions: the frame behind the pilot's back was provided with 8.5 mm thick armour.

From an external point of view, two other elements characterised the La-5 (as well as the subsequent La-7): the two mobile bulkheads arranged along the sides of the fuselage which allowed the heat dissipation by the engine to be modulated and the positioning of the dynamic intake for the oil radiator which, varying according to the engine version, also allowed the aircraft version to be identified at a quick glance.

- The horizontal tail was cantilevered, the stabilizer had two spars, entirely made of wood, with plywood covering.

The stabilizer consisted of two halves, attached to the power elements of the tail section of the fuselage, while the trimmer elevator had a fabric-covered duralumin frame and was also made of two halves.

- The landing gear was retractable, double-supported, with tail wheel.

The main mounts were equipped with oleopneumatic shock absorbers. The main wheels, 650x200 mm, were equipped with air-chamber brakes. The freely orientable tail mount was retracted into the fuselage and was equipped with a 300x125 mm wheel.

- The aircraft had mixed control: the ailerons were controlled by rigid rods, while the elevator and rudder were controlled by cables.

The flaps were released and retracted by hydraulic means.
The propulsion plant consisted of an air-cooled M-82 radial engine and a VISh-105V three-bladed variable-pitch propeller with a diameter of 3.1 m .
Engine temperature was regulated by front fins located in the front ring of the hood and two fins on the sides of the hood, behind the engine.

The oil cooler was honeycomb-shaped and was positioned under the engine, in the tunnel of the lower bonnet cover: at the exit, the tunnel was equipped with an adjustable valve.

- The engine was started with compressed air.

The 59-litre oil tank was located in the fuselage, at the junction between the wooden part and the metal truss.
The fuel capacity of 539 litres was divided into three central tanks and two tanks in the console.

- The armament consisted of two synchronized ShVAK SP-20 cannons, caliber 20 mm, with a total ammunition capacity of 340 rounds, with pneumatic and mechanical reloading and a PBP-la collimator.
- In some cases the possibility of installing a third cannon is indicated.
- According to some, the last examples built were equipped with 23 mm caliber weapons, as would later happen with the La-7.

Among the offensive loads for use in ground attack missions, the various sources found report the possibility of carrying bombs but indicate different values, indicated from time to time as 100 kg, 150 kg or 200 kg.
In the La-5NF version, special underwing racks allowed the aircraft to carry four 82 mm rockets as an alternative to bombs.
In addition to the standard set of flight, navigation and control instruments, the equipment included a RSI-4 shortwave radio station, an oxygen device and a landing light.

- The La-5FN aircraft were equipped with KPA-3bis or KP-12 oxygen devices: the oxygen supply was sufficient for a 1.5-hour flight at an altitude of 8,000 meters.

The plant guaranteed that the service life of the M-82 before repair was 100 hours, but in reality the service life was less: due to the poor fit of the piston pairs and rings, oil accumulated in the combustion chambers of the lower cylinders, the engine emitted smoke and covered the entire fuselage with soot.

- But, if not all the accumulated oil was expelled through the exhaust pipes, a strong shock occurred in the compression stroke and, as a result, the connecting rod broke or the cylinder head was destroyed.

The VG-12 candles used on the M-82 lasted 5 hours, and during periods of heavy combat, a La-5 required 14 candles per day.
The problem lay in the unfortunate shape of the cylinder heads: the spark plugs were constantly immersed in oil, which made them sooty, and lead from the petrol was deposited on the soot.

- Early La-5s, like the LaGG-3, did not have slats and had a tendency to stall on their wings.

Resolution No. 1895ss of the State Defense Committee of June 7, 1942 called for the introduction of mechanization of the wing leading edge on the LaGG-3 and La-5 starting from July 1, but by the end of the first ten days of July this had been done only on the 7th LaGG-3 and the 8th La-5.

- Only in August did all aircraft begin to be produced with slats.

In the summer of 1942, work was carried out on the La-5 to improve the tightness of the hatches and doors of the chassis.
On July 24, the NKAP and the Air Force had issued order No. 559a/s/032 on the use of armor on fighters.
Initially, the La-5 was fitted with armored glass and introduced fuel tank protection. In addition, the same document defined the use of a red-illuminated aiming grid on the La-5 fighters and a button-type electro-pneumatic trigger for the guns like that of the Me-109, instead of the traditional mechanical triggers.
By order of the People's Commissariat for Aviation Industry No. 605 of August 8, starting from August 10, each La-5 was to

be equipped with an RSI-4 radio receiver and transmitter, as well as an RPK-10 radio compass.

- Although it was not possible to meet the set deadline (2 days), things nevertheless moved forward and the Soviet fighters began to receive radio navigation and communication equipment.

By the end of 1942, Gorky began producing the La-5 with a significantly modified nose section: the double skin disappeared completely, the fuselage became lighter, and labor intensity was reduced. On the recommendation of TsAGI, meanwhile, an exhaust had been installed on the rear frame of the sliding part of the canopy, smoothing out the difference in height between the cabin and the fairing.

- The kinematics of the tail support were also modified: now the wheel was pulled higher and the flaps did not protrude beyond the contour of the tail section.

In December 1942, production of the La-5 began at Plant No. 31 in Tbilisi, where production of the LaGG-3 also continued. By the end of the year, this plant had built 22 new fighters and delivered another 5 early the following year.
However, the 1943 plan for this undertaking envisaged increasing the production of LaG-5 by 1.5 times, while improving its performance characteristics.
The first aviation regiments armed with this fighter appeared at the front in the autumn of 1942, near Stalingrad.
The La-5 quickly gained recognition.
Pilots liked not only its high performance and powerful armament, two ShVAK cannons, but also the air-cooled engine, which had a longer life than a liquid-cooled engine and at the same time protected against enemy fire from the front.

Cockpit

1. Clock
2. Relative speed indicator
3. Tachometer
4. Fuel level indicator
5. Altimeter
6. Magnetic compass
7. Manometer manifold
8. Fuel pressure (left), oil temperature (center), oil pressure (right)
9. Compass Repeater
10. Turn indicator
11. Variometer
12. Engine temperature indicator

13. Gear Level
14. Motor magnet position
15. Landing gear position indicator: green: down - no light: in transition - red: up
16. External Ordnance Status Light
17. Flap lever
18. Engine mixture: rear position: leaner mixture - front position: richer mixture
19. Gas knob
20. Propeller pitch lever
21. Boost lever: rear position: stage 1 - front position: stage 2

Versions

- **LaG-5**

Also called La-5, it was the first production version, essentially an adaptation of the structure of the previous LaGG-3 to the M-82 engine.

- **La-5F**

Powered by an improved version of the M-82 engine, it introduced modifications to the wings and fuselage. The latter allowed the pilot to have a 360° view.

- **La-5F TK-3**

Three prototypes built using aircraft from the previous series, on which a turbocharged version of the M-82 engine was installed. Evaluated for high-altitude use, they did not lead to series production due to the increase in weight which effectively cancelled out the advantages obtained from supercharging the engine.

- **La-5 M-71**

It was a single prototype, equipped with a Shvetsov M-71 engine, an 18-cylinder radial engine, derived from the Shvetsov M-25, itself a license-produced version of the American Wright R-1820.
The aircraft, although potentially promising, did not see any follow-up due to the poor availability of the engine and the

reluctance to proceed with the overhaul of the assembly lines recently set up for the production of the La-5F version.

- **La-5FN**

Substantially revised version in the structure which, from entirely wooden, became mixed, with the introduction of metal longerons in the fuselage.
Equipped with the injection version of the M-82 engine, it benefited from the significant increase in power, expressing remarkable performances that made it one of the aircraft most feared by the enemy.

- **S-95**

This was the definition given by the Czechoslovakian air forces to the La-5FNs used from the final stages of the Second World War.

- **The-5UTI**

Two-seater version, intended for training.
Stripped of the starboard cannon, the armoured glass in the roof, the armoured backrest, the radio equipment, the oxygen system, the inert gas system in the tank and the bomb racks.
It was produced in a limited series because, in the trainer role, the Yakovlev Yak-7V was preferred.

Shvetsov M-82 engine

The Shvetsov ASH-82, also referred to as the M-82, was a 14-cylinder twin-row air-cooled radial aircraft engine designed by OKB 19 under Arkady Dmitrievich Shvecov and developed in the Soviet Union in the late 1930s and early 1940s.

- Minimum permissible cylinder temperature for operation: 120°C.
- Maximum permissible cylinder temperature: 250°C.
- Maximum allowable cruising temperature: 225°C.
- Normal temperature of the cylinders in cruise: 160 to 180°C

Arkadiy Shvetsov developed the ASH-82 design from the Wright Cyclone, but reduced its size and weight.
Developed from the Shvetsov M-62, itself a development of the single-star M-25, a license-produced version of the American Wright R-1820 Cyclone, it was supplied to some Soviet-produced fighter models in service during World War II.
In terms of characteristics, the M-82 was superior to the best examples of foreign engines.

- For example, the BMW-801 engine did not enter production until 1942 and had less power and more weight than the M-82.

More than 70,000 units were produced.

Versions

- **ASh-82-111 (M-82-111)**

First mass-produced ASh-82, equipped with carburetor power and supercharging with a single-stage, two-speed compressor. Power:

- 1,570 hp (1,170 kW) at 2,400 rpm at take-off.
- 1,540 hp (1,148 kW) at 2,400 rpm at 2,000 meters (6,600 ft).
- 1,330 hp (992 kW) at 2,400 rpm at 5,500 meters (18,000 feet).
- 820 hp (612 kW) at 2,400 rpm at 8,500 meters (27,900 ft).

This version suffered from lubrication problems and carburetor ice formation in extremely cold conditions.

- **ASh-82-112 (M-82-112)**

Development of the M-82-111 featuring a longer scheduled maintenance interval and increased reliability.
The carburetors, the lubrication system, the gears of the reduction gear between the shaft and the propeller hub, the turbocharger and the OHV distribution system were redesigned. The new version managed to improve the overall characteristics of the engine in the harsh Russian winter.

- **ASh-82F (M-82F)**

Substantially identical to the previous ASh-82, except for a further extended scheduled maintenance interval, as well as an improved lubrication system, which allowed constant operation at maximum power, with carburettors:

- 1,650 hp (1,230 kW) at 2,400 rpm for take-off.
- 1,430 hp (1,067 kW) at 2,400 rpm at 5,000 meters (16,000 ft) .

- 800 hp (597 kW) at 2,400 rpm at 10,000 meters (33,000 ft).

Thus, up to an altitude of 1,500-1,600 meters, the engine had over 200 hp more in combat conditions.

- **ASh-82FN (M-82FN)**

ASH-82F direct injection, with power increased to 1,850 hp at take-off, with an increase of only 30 kg in engine weight.

- 1,850 hp (1,380 kW) at 2,500 rpm for take-off.
- 1,650 hp (1,230 kW) at 2,400 rpm at 1,650 meters (5,410 ft).
- 1,450 hp (1,082 kW) at 2,400 rpm at 4,650 meters (15,260 ft).
- 810 hp (604 kW) at 2,400 rpm at 10,500 meters (34,400 ft).

Engine weight increase of only 30 kg.

- **ASH-82FNU (M-82FNU)**

Improved M-82FN with higher boost pressure and rpm: power increased to 1,850 hp. After all these improvements, the ASH-82FN and ASH-82FNU proved to be two of the most robust engines of the war.

Lavochkin La-7

The Lavochkin La-7 was a single-engine, low-wing fighter designed by OKB 301 under Semyon Alekseevič Lavochkin and developed in the Soviet Union in the 1940s.
The final development of the original LaGG-1, it was used mainly by the VVS in the final stages of World War II, remaining operational until the 1950s.
Over 6,000 examples were produced, and by the end of 1943 the La-7 was considered probably the best dogfighting fighter in service in the world, selected by most of the greatest VVS aces.
A small batch of La-7s were given to the Czechoslovak Air Force, but were otherwise not exported.

- The La-7 was considered by pilots to be on par with the best German fighters and even shot down a Messerschmitt Me 262.

It was decommissioned from the Soviet Air Force in 1947, but remained in service in Czechoslovakia until 1950.

- The fruit of intensive research by the TsAGI on the Lavochkin La-5, the La-7 appeared in early 1944.

Its lightweight structure included metal wing spars, a third 20 mm cannon, and aerodynamic improvements that increased the aircraft's maximum speed to 680 km/h, some 30 km/h faster than its predecessor the La-5FN.
Pilots considered the La-7 at least on par with all German piston-engined fighters.
The first example of the La-7 appeared in late 1943 and entered service with units in early 1944.

- The La-7, powered by a more powerful M-82FNU or M-82FNV engine, was armed with two or three 23 mm cannon and six 82 mm rockets.

Externally it differed from the La-5 by the modified cabin and the oil radiator relocated under the fuselage, behind the trailing edge.

Lavochkin La-7.

Also built in series was a liaison and training model, the La-7UTI, as well as two La-7R fighters equipped with liquid-fueled rocket boosters in the tail.

- This latest version reached a maximum speed of over 800 km/h, at 3,500 metres.

However, it was not built due to attacks on the wooden structure caused by rocket fuel fumes: furthermore, the additional stresses imposed on the cell limited its potential use in the absence of reinforcement.

They were excellent low- and medium-altitude fighters, fast and well-armed, rustic but perfectly capable of outmaneuvering the

latest German fighters, with the greatest chance of victory at their altitude of operation.
The two greatest Russian aces of World War II, Ivan Kojedub (62 victories) and Alexandr Pokryshin (59 victories), became such while piloting Lavochkin fighters, which they flew for almost their entire operational careers.

History

The Lavochkin La-7 fighter is a classic example of how the life of an aircraft can be extended by intelligently modifying its aerodynamic qualities and installing increasingly more powerful engines.

But, while this evolution usually occurs at the expense of the aircraft's original piloting capabilities, the La-7, on the contrary, benefited from it to the point of establishing itself as one of the Soviet Union's best fighters during World War II.

- The Lavochkin La-7 was basically an improved version, aerodynamically and aesthetically, of the Lavochkin La-5.

The massive upper air intake had been removed and the oil cooler and supercharger were fed by intakes in the wing roots and under the fuselage.

However, due to the relocation of the oil radiator under the fuselage, the oil pipes had to be laid directly under the pilot's feet, which is why the normal temperature in the cockpit was +40° C in winter, while in summer it increased to +55°.

The most important improvement over the La-5, however, was the construction of the wing structure in aluminium alloy, rather than wood: by 1943 there was no longer the terrible shortage of strategic materials of the previous years and Lavockhin was able to revise his project using better materials.

In fact, the replacement of the wooden wing spars with duralumin ones reduced the weight by 100 kg.

- The new M.82FN engine now delivered 1,850 hp.

The La-7 was first flight-tested in the second half of 1943 , with operational tests beginning early the following year.

- In July 1944 the first production batch was assigned to the 176th Fighter Regiment of the VVS.

Each engine cylinder was given its own exhaust pipe, the engine cowling shrouds were reduced in number, a rollbar was added to the cockpit, longer main landing gear shock absorbers were fitted while the tailwheel shock absorber was shortened, an improved PB-1B(V) gunsight was installed, and a new VISh-105V-4 propeller was fitted.

- In addition to the excellent flight characteristics, the tests also revealed a number of shortcomings: the hydraulic system often failed and there were interruptions in engine operation.

This last defect remained the real scourge of the La-7 until the end of the war: it was connected with the relocation of the air intakes from the engine cowling to the wing roots, places most vulnerable to the ingress of dust during take-off and landing, dust and earth particles leading to engine failure.

- In the frost when the La-7 was subjected to state tests, there was no dust at the airfields, therefore, it was not possible to identify the defect in time.

An attempt to get rid of the defect was the installation of filters on the air intakes and the appearance of additional air intakes on the lower surface of the wings, in front of the main landing gear wheel cleaning wells.

- The La-7 proved not only to be 70 km/h faster than the Focke-Wulf Fw 190, but could out-climb and out-turn both the Fw 190 and the Messerschmitt Bf 109.

Many regiments were enthusiastic about the idea of replacing their liquid-cooled Yaks with the radial-engined, air-cooled La-7s, which were not only superior in flying qualities but were also better able to withstand the temperature extremes of the Russian winter and summer.

- Its speed of 680 km/h, greater operational range and superior rate of climb soon made it the aircraft of choice for the greatest Soviet aces.

Major Sultan Amet-Khan, already an ace of the "Russian" Hawker Hurricanes, with a total of 30 individual kills and 19 in tandem, achieved many of his victories on the La-7.
Even the Soviet Union's most successful ace in what is known in Russia as the "Great Patriotic War", Ivan Nikitovich Kozhedub, nicknamed "Ivan the Terrible", three times Hero of the Soviet Union, achieved his last 17 victories in 1945, precisely with a La-7.

- The last aircraft he shot down was a German jet fighter, the Messerschmitt Me 262, Sergeant Kurt Lange of the 1st Squadron, 54th Wing, in the skies of Frankfurt an der Oder, again aboard a La-7.

The La-7 had a climb time to 5,000 meters of about 4 minutes, perhaps a little better than the earlier La-5.
The model had, despite a more powerful engine, also an increased armament by a third 20 mm cannon installed in the nose, firing through the propeller disk thanks to the synchronizer, with a certain, inevitable, loss of rate of fire.
It was used mainly as an escort fighter, rarely as a fighter-bomber.
Production of the La-7 continued until the end of 1945, a total of 6,158 vehicles were built:

- NKAP Plant No. 21 in Gorky built 4,610 aircraft.
- Moscow Plant No. 381 built 1,298 of them.
- Plant No. 99 in Ulan-Ude produced 250 fighters.

With this machine, equivalent to the Yak-9U, Soviet pilots had a contender against the best German fighters and in any conditions.
Armament consisted of two or three 20 mm automatic cannon, equipped with a hydromechanical synchronizer that prevented the shells from entering the propeller blades.

- Most La-7 fighters were armed with two 20 mm ShVAK cannons with 200 rounds each.

A relatively small number of La-7s received the originally intended standard armament of three B-20 guns with 170 rounds of ammunition each.
The reliability of the B-20 gun was lower than required, which was confirmed by tests of the three-point La-7 at the Air Force Research Institute from 10 September to 10 October 1945.
Of the three aircraft, serial numbers 45214414, 45214415, 45214416, that took part in the tests, none managed to reach the required figure of 5,000 rounds fired from one aircraft without shell failures:

- On the first fighter, this figure was 3,275 shells.
- On the second of 3,222.
- On the third of 3,155.

An attempt to radically solve the reliability problems of the B-20 guns was the installation of a 23 mm NS-23 cannon on the La-7: the aircraft with the new weapon was tested from 20 to 31 July 1945, but the results were again disappointing: the weapon functioned unreliably.

Lavochkin La-7.

- Repeated tests of the La-7 fighter armed with NS-23 cannons, which took place from 2 to 10 October 1945, were more successful and the NS-23 cannon, together with the B-20, was put into service.

Several La-7s received onboard armament of three ShVAK cannons with 130 rounds of ammunition each, but these aircraft proved to be overloaded, as the weight of one ShVAK cannon in the powered version was 44.5 kg, while the weight of the B-20 cannon was only 25 kg.

- The initial velocity of the projectile fired from the ShVAK cannon is 215 m/s with a rate of fire of 800 rounds/min.

Production of the first aircraft equipped with three B-20 guns began in January 1945, when 74 were delivered.

- These aircraft were 65 kg (143 lb) heavier than those with the two ShVAK guns, but level flight speed was slightly improved over the original aircraft.

However, the time to climb to 5,000 metres (16,000 ft) increased by two-tenths of a second over the previous model.
The ammunition kit included armor-piercing incendiary shells weighing 180 grams, capable of penetrating armor up to 20 mm thick, and fragmentation incendiary shells weighing 180 grams.
On two underwing nodes it was possible to suspend bombs weighing up to 100 kg each: the most frequently used high-explosive bombs were the FAB-50 and FAB-100, as well as the incendiary ZAB-50 and ZAB-100, weighing 0 kg and 100 kg respectively.

Use

The 63rd Guards Fighter Aviation Regiment (GIAP) began combat trials of the La-7 in mid-September 1944 in support of the 1st Baltic Front. Thirty aircraft were supplied for the month-long trials. During this period the new fighters flew 462 individual sorties and claimed 55 aerial victories, losing four aircraft in combat.

Four more La-7s were lost to non-combat causes, mostly related to engine problems.

A total of three pilots were killed during testing from all causes.

The commander of the 63rd GIAP regiment, Colonel Yevgeny Gorbatyuk, a Hero of the Soviet Union, commented:

"The La-7 has shown indisputable advantages over German aircraft in multiple air combats. In addition to fighter tasks, photo reconnaissance and bombing were successfully undertaken. The aircraft surpasses the La-5FN in speed, maneuverability and, above all, in landing characteristics. It requires changes in its armament and urgent repair of its engine."

The dual ShVAK armament inherited from the La-5 was no longer powerful enough to shoot down later, more heavily armoured German fighters, especially the Focke-Wulf Fw 190, in a single burst, even when Soviet pilots opened fire at ranges of only 50–100 metres (160–330 ft).

The 156th Fighter Aviation Regiment of the 4th Air Army was the next unit to receive the La-7 in October 1944.

At one point during the month, they had fourteen aircraft simultaneously unserviceable due to engine failures.

- On January 1, 1945, there were 398 La-7s in front-line service, of which 107 were unserviceable.
- By 9 May 1945, this number had increased to 967 aircraft, of which only 169 were unserviceable.

For the invasion of Japanese Manchuria, 313 La-7s were assigned and only 28 of these were unserviceable on 9 August 1945.

The La-7 was flown by the top Soviet ace of the war, Ivan Nikitovich Kozhedub, and was successfully used by him to shoot down an Me 262 jet fighter, one of the few such kills of the war.

Kozhedub, three times Hero of the Soviet Union, achieved his last 17 air victories in 1945 on La-7 number 27, which is now preserved in the Central Air Force Museum in Monino on the outskirts of Moscow.

A fighter regiment of the 1st Czechoslovak Composite Aviation Division was later equipped with the La-7 after participating in the Slovak National Uprising of August–October 1944 with the La-5FN.

- A total of 56 aircraft were delivered, which equipped the 1st and 2nd Fighter Regiments.

Most of the aircraft, however, were delivered in 1945, and saw no combat during the war, remaining in service with the Czechoslovakians until 1950 and being designated post-war by them as the S-97.

One of these aircraft survives in the Aviation Museum in Prague.

- Despite reports to the contrary, no La-7 was ever sold or transferred to the People's Republic of China or North Korea.

Such reports arose from misidentification by Western pilots of La-9s or La-11s that had been issued to those countries.
British test pilot Eric Brown had the chance to fly a La-7 at the former Luftwaffe Erprobungsstelle Tarnewitz aircraft testing station on the Baltic coast, shortly after the German surrender in May 1945.
He described the handling and performance as "quite superb", but the armament and sights were "below average", the "wooden construction would have withstood little punishment in combat" and the instrumentation was "appallingly basic".
The La-7 ended the superiority in vertical maneuverability that the Messerschmitt Bf 109G had previously enjoyed over other Soviet fighters.

- Furthermore, it was fast enough at low altitude to reach, albeit with some difficulty, the Focke-Wulf Fw 190 fighter-bombers attacking Soviet units on the front line and immediately return to German-controlled airspace at full speed.

The Yakovlev Yak-3 and Yakovlev Yak-9U with the Klimov VK-107 engine did not have a large enough speed margin to outrun the German raiders.
In total, 115 La-7s were lost in air combat, only half the number of Yak-3s.
According to VVS records, only three La-7s were actually shot down in aerial combat in all of 1944 and only 10 fell victim to anti-aircraft fire with another 23 from non-combat related causes.

- Air combat losses in 1945 amounted to 79 in total.

However, aircraft that disappeared, or, in any case, did not return, or were lost due to wear and tear are not included, such as, for example, 24 additional La-7s that disappeared in 1944.

However, VVS loss totals may not provide a true picture of combat losses, as combat losses were often declared as non-combat losses to conceal the losses themselves or for propaganda purposes.

Versions

- **La-7**

Main series version.

- **La-7TK**

Experimental version used to evaluate the TK-3 turbocharger, built in July 1944 in the hope of improving high-altitude performance.
It was destroyed on a test flight when the turbocharger disintegrated.

- **La-7R**

Test stand for a tail-mounted RD-1KhZ liquid-fuel rocket engine. The rocket was rated at 300 kg thrust and its fuel, 90 liters of kerosene and 170 liters of nitric acid, was expected to last between three and three and a half minutes.
While the rocket was operating, it increased the fighter's speed by 80 kilometres per hour (50 mph), but the aircraft's other flying qualities deteriorated.
It reached 785 km/h at 13,000 metres, but the cell was made of wood and was at risk of corroding due to the acids used by the engine, which was located in the tail.

- Version made in a single copy.

Fifteen flights were made in the first quarter of 1945, although the rocket exploded on the ground on 12 May: the aircraft was repaired, but later suffered an in-flight explosion, although the pilot managed to land safely. Details of any subsequent flights are unknown, but the La-7R was exhibited at Tushino.

- **La-7PVRD**

Test bed for two underwing ramjet engines.
Experimental version with the new VRD ramjet, capable of delivering 300 kg of thrust, tested on various types of Soviet aircraft.
The aircraft was expected to reach a speed of 800 km/h (497 mph) at an altitude of 6,000 metres (19,685 ft), but could not exceed 670 km/h (416 mph) due to the high aerodynamic drag of the ramjets.
However, testing was completed in 1946, by which time it was already obsolete due to the new jet age.
Version made in a single copy.

- **La-7/M-71**

Experimental version equipped with a Shvetsov M-71 engine, conversion carried out in 1944.
Flight tests determined that the engine was not yet fully developed for series production and the program was cancelled.

- **La-120R**

Further evolution of the La-7, with a 1,900 hp engine and a laminar flow wing, RD-1KhZ engine, reduction of fuel capacity on board from 296 to 215 liters and a total increase in overall weight of 100 kg.
It reached 805 km/h, compared to 725 km/h with the piston engine alone, but there were a couple of explosions on board which caused the end of the program in 1944.

- **The-7UTI**

Two-seater training version.
Armament reduced to a single 20 mm cannon and the oil cooler was relocated under the engine cowling.
Equipped with radio compass and gun camera.
Considerably heavier than the fighter, 3,500 kg (7,716 lb), but retained the flying characteristics of the single-seater aircraft.
584 examples were built, the last two delivered in 1947.

Technical features

Dimensions and weights

- Length: 8.67 meters
- Wingspan: 9.80 meters
- Height: 2.54 meters
- Wing area: 17.59 m^2
- Empty weight: 2,605 kg
- Maximum take-off weight: 3,265 kg

Propulsion

- Engine: a radial Shvetsov As h-82FN
- Power: 1,850 hp (1,361 kW)

Performance

- Maximum speed: 597 km/h at sea level - 680 km/h at altitude
- Climb rate: 18.52 meters per second
- Autonomy: 635 km
- Tangency: 10,750 meters

Armament

- Guns: two 20 mm ShVAKs with 200 rounds each or three 20 mm Berezin B-20s with 130 rounds each
- Bombs: 200 kg

Berezin B-20

The Berezin B-20 was a 20 mm automatic cannon used by Soviet aircraft during World War II.
The B-20 was created by Mikhail Y. Berezin in 1944 by converting his 12.7 mm Berezin UB machine gun to use the 20 mm shells used by the ShVAK cannon.

- No other changes were made to the weapon which was either pneumatically or mechanically loaded and was available in both synchronized and non-synchronized versions.

In 1946, an electric-fire version was created for the turrets of the Tupolev Tu-4 bomber until the Nudelman-Rikhter NR-23 cannon became available.
The B-20 was a welcome replacement for the ShVAK because it was significantly lighter, only 25 kg (55 lb) compared to the ShVAK's 40 kg (80 lb), all without sacrificing rate of fire or muzzle velocity.

- Rate of fire is 800 rounds/min, 600 rounds/min for the synchronized version.

Lavochkin La-7R

Test stand for a tail-mounted RD-1KhZ liquid-fuel rocket engine. The rocket was rated at 300 kg thrust and its fuel, 90 liters of kerosene and 170 liters of nitric acid, was expected to last between three and three and a half minutes.

While the rocket was operating, it increased the fighter's speed by 80 kilometres per hour (50 mph), but the aircraft's other flying qualities deteriorated.

- It reached 785 km/h at 13,000 metres, but the cell was made of wood and was at risk of corroding due to the acids used by the engine, which was located in the tail.

By September 1944, the decision of the State Defense Committee was to build and submit for flight tests modifications of the Yak-9, La-7 and Su-6 2TK-3 fighters with additional RD-1 rocket engines developed by V. P. Glushko in the NKVD design bureau at Plant No. 16.

- When operating the boosters on the Yak-9 and La-7 aircraft, the climb time to 5,000 meters was to be reduced to three minutes, and the maximum horizontal flight speed was to be increased to 780 km/h in a time interval of up to three minutes.

SA Lavochkin entrusted the execution of this task to the branch of the design bureau organized in March 1944 in Moscow, which was headed by SM Alekseev.

The branch was called "Experimental Plant No. 81" and was located in a part of the Moscow Serial Aircraft Plant No. 381 specially allocated to it, which at that time produced the La-7 aircraft.

The modification of the first serial La-7, which received the new name La-7R-1, was completed by 21 October 1944.

- On this aircraft, and the La-7R-2 that followed it, the tail section of the fuselage was finalized to house the RD-1 within it.

The center gas tank was replaced by a nitric acid reserve, while a kerosene tank was installed in the starboard wing console.
The nitric acid stock was 270 kg, the kerosene stock was 60 kg, while the gasoline stock was reduced from 340 to 210 kg.
This amount of fuel was sufficient to operate the RD-1 for 3.5 - 3.8 minutes.
To supply fuel components to the RD-1 combustion chamber, a pump was used, driven by a special shaft frictionally connected to a ratchet, on the rear cover of the ASh-82FN engine.
In the nitric acid and kerosene tanks, a pressure of 40-50 atm was provided with pressure in the engine combustion chamber up to 23 atmospheres.

- Control of the rocket engine was fully automated and consisted only of the use of the throttle handle and the starting air tap.

To prevent corrosion, which even a small amount of acid fumes led to, the aircraft structure had been carefully insulated.
Factory tests of the La-7R-1 began on 27 October 1944.
In early November, two flights were made to test the propeller group (VMG) without igniting the rocket engine.
During subsequent ground tests of the RD-1, it was found that the torque generated by the transmission from the ASH-82FN to the LRE pump unit was insufficient.
After the defect was eliminated, flight testing continued.
Three flights were devoted to the development of repeated firings of the liquid-fuel rocket engine.

In the first of these, the engine failed completely; in the second, after the first launch, it worked for 15 seconds and when repeated, it failed; in the third, in two launches, the RD-1 worked for 15 seconds, but failed with another launch attempt. The cause of the failures could not be established.

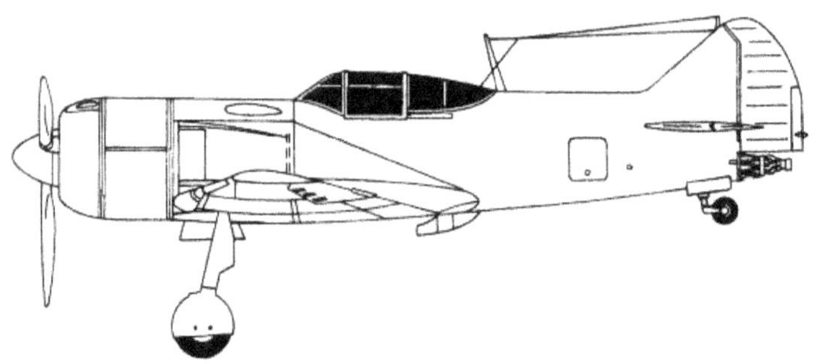

Project of a La-7R with rocket mounting in the rear: October 1944.

In three further flights, maximum horizontal speeds were determined at an altitude of 3,000 metres in the nominal operating mode of the ASH-82FN with LRE at idle and operating.

- In the third, most successful flight, the speed increase due to the operation of the RD-1 was 85 km/h.

Factory testing of the program was completed on February 24, 1945, and the aircraft was placed under repair.
In total, test pilot AV Davydov performed 15 flights, including five with the inclusion of the RD-1.
The second copy of the La-7R-2 was built at the 81st plant, mainly from La-7 units of the 51st series.
Unlike the La-7R-1, which was merely a flying laboratory, this aircraft had better aerodynamics.

In 1945, the La-7R-2 entered flight tests: from January 26 to March 27, 19 flights were performed, 45 LRE launches, including six in the air.

In two RD-1 launches, the platforms were removed in flight.

On March 1, at an altitude of 2,700 meters, the engine ran for a minute and a half, after which, due to pulsations in the combustion chamber, it had to be turned off.

The speed increase was 80 km/h on the instrument and on March 10, at an altitude of 2,600 meters, the RD-1 added about 95 km/h of increase.

- Overall the engine performed poorly, failing 15 times out of 45 starts, and in 6 cases due to an ignition failure.

On March 27, during a test flight on the La-7 flying at an altitude of 6,000 meters, the additional engine did not ignite, an attempt to restart at an altitude of 3,000 meters ended with a strong explosion in the combustion chamber of the RD-1.

The rudders were severely damaged, the plane lost control and overturned.

By April 14, the damaged empennage and combustion chamber on the La-7 were replaced, and minor defects that appeared as a result of the accident were eliminated.

- The aircraft was equipped with an RD-1 engine, which has special diaphragms, with a hole up to 20 mm in diameter, to ensure pressure from ether-air ignition to the ground at 0.5 atmospheres.

However, attempts to launch it at altitudes of 5,000–6,000 meters ended in vain. Due to the large number of RD-1 failures associated with ignition problems, the OKB-SD of Plant No. 16 developed a version of the RD-1X3 engine with chemical ignition instead of electrical ignition.

The following fuel components were used as starting fuel components: B23-75 fuel, a synthetic rubber intermediate solution in B-70 gasoline, and an oxidizing agent, nitric acid.
Installation of the RD-1X3 on the La-7 began on April 29, however, the RD-1X3 was no more reliable than its predecessor: accidents continued.
The next day, May 12, during ground fire tests on the La-7, the engine combustion chamber exploded.
Of the four RD-1X3s assembled and flight-tested, three crashed, while the fourth, intended for the Su-6, was received only on 11 May and mounted on the aircraft.

- The last of the remaining RD-1X3s was sent to OKB-16 for overhaul.

Laboratory studies have shown that the explosions were caused by hydraulic shocks in the combustion chamber, which occurred as a result of a sharp increase in pressure in the combustion chamber "jackets" at the moment of opening the fuel valves.
The hydraulic shock damaged the ignition device, there was an accumulation of components inside the chamber, the subsequent ignition of which led to an explosion.
Three RD-1X3 engines of a new modification for the Yak-3, La-7 and Su-6 aircraft arrived as early as July 14, 1945.
They were equipped with special start and exhaust valves, and the injectors of both fuel components were switched in series, which significantly increased the ignition efficiency, which, in fact, made the engine start without problems.
The engine was installed on the La-7R-2 on 25 July.
14 flights were performed on this aircraft in the period up to 16 September 1945.
Of the 49 engine starts, 8 were made in the air.
The RD-1X3 failed 23 times, but only two failures were caused by the ignition altitude.

Despite all the difficulties, the tests were, however, completed: on the La-7R, a maximum flight speed of 795 km/h was achieved at an altitude of 6300 meters.

Technical features

Dimensions

- Wingspan: 9.80 meters
- Wing area: 17.59 m^2
- Length: 8.67 meters

Propeller

- An alternative engine «Shvecov» ASh-82FN + booster engine RD-1X3
- Thrust: 300 kg

Weights

- Empty weight: 2,703 kg
- Full load weight: 3,500 kg

Performance

- Maximum speed: 795 km/h at 6,300 meters
- Tangency: 13,000 meters
- Maximum rate of climb: 1,340 m/min

Armament

- 2 x 20 mm ShVAK cannons

Lavochkin La-9

The Lavochkin La-9 was a single-engine, low-wing fighter designed by OKB 301 under Semyon Alekseevič Lavochkin and developed in the Soviet Union in the second half of the 1940s.

- Derived from the previous La-7, it failed to be developed in time for use during the Second World War.

Later, a new variant, the La-11, was developed from the La-9, intended for long-range escort.
The La-9 was the metal version of the earlier Lavochkin La-7: in reality it was completely redesigned, with many innovations, so much so that in the end it resembled its German contemporary Fw 190D.
The structure was now metal, except for the fabric covering of the ailerons, and a twin-spar laminar flow wing.
The rear part of the fuselage was connected to the cockpit canopy and not lowered behind it as on the La-7, thus not allowing a full rear view.

- The weight savings, due to the metal construction, allowed for increased fuel capacity and an armament of four 23 mm NS-23 cannon.

The new fighter entered production in August 1946 and by the end of production in 1948, 1,559 aircraft had been built.
Even with the overall reduction in size, especially in the fuselage surface area, the La-9 was heavier than its predecessor.
In fact, it adopted a finally metallic structure, which imposed a certain increase in the overall mass, while giving obvious advantages to the durability and vulnerability of the aircraft.

The machine was also greatly enhanced in its armament, consisting of 4 23 mm caliber cannons, as always grouped in the nose to give a very concentrated volume of fire, also because, on the other hand, there was no space for weapons in the wing.

Lavochkin La-9 at the Warbirds Over Wanaka airshow, Wanaka, New Zealand, 2006.

The engine was an AshV-82FN, improved over its predecessors which had the earlier M-82.

It remained in service for a long time, proving to be an excellent low and medium altitude fighter, nicknamed "Fritz" by the Allies.

He served in various countries, such as Korea and China, where he was also employed in combat.

On the rear wall of the wing were mounted Fries-type ailerons with fabric covering and uncontrolled trimmers, as well as landing flaps with a deflection angle of up to 60 °, positioned between the fuselage and the ailerons.

- The front part, with a more spacious cabin than the La-7, and the rear parts of the fuselage were joined together by four bolted joints.

The pilot's canopy consisted of a front armoured glass, a movable central section and a rear section: the central section was opened and closed by a mechanism mounted on the starboard side and was equipped with an emergency release device during flight.

The tail consisted of a vertical stabilizer, made in a single piece with the fuselage, and a rudder, while the free horizontal support tail, with a symmetrical profile, consisted of two stabilizing consoles with elevators.

Horizontal tail installation angle: + 1°: On production vehicles, this angle has been increased to +1.5°.

The elevator and rudder, with metal frame and fabric covering, had aerodynamic compensation and weight balance.

- To reduce the effort required to operate the control elements, they were equipped with trims.

The powerplant was a 14-cylinder double-star air-cooled radial engine ASH-82FN with a two-speed supercharger and a three-bladed propeller VISH-105V-4 with a diameter of 3.1 meters.

The engine cooling air intakes were located in the front engine ring, while two side fins were located on the sides of the hood behind the engine.

- The oil radiator was located under the fuselage, in a tunnel, at the exit of which was an adjustable valve.

The intake manifold was positioned above the engine, between the gun barrels, and did not extend beyond the contours of the bonnet: the intake manifolds were positioned in the front ring of the bonnet, while a dust filter was installed in the intake pipe.

The all-metal construction of the airframe made it possible to increase the number of fuel tanks to five, for a total capacity of 850 litres: the tanks were located in the centre section and in the wings.

- The 63-liter oil tank was only filled to 50 liters.

The aircraft was equipped with four synchronized NS-23 cannons with 300 rounds of ammunition.
It should be noted that the La-9, equipped with one of the best guns, was rightly considered the most heavily armed piston-engined fighter.

- Fire control was pneumatic-electric, which allowed either separate firing of the two upper guns or the two lower guns, or a salvo from all four.

On production vehicles, the PBP(V) type sight, installed under the canopy, was replaced with the ASP-1N, created by OKB-16, which was a copy of the English MK-2D, used on fighters supplied to the USSR during the war.
The aircraft was controlled by a mixed system: the elevator and ailerons were controlled by sticks, while the rudder was controlled by cables.
One example, designated La-138, was equipped with two 300 kg thrust PVRD-430 ramjets under the wings: factory tests were performed between March and April 1947 and speed increases from 107 to 112 km/h in level flight were recorded.

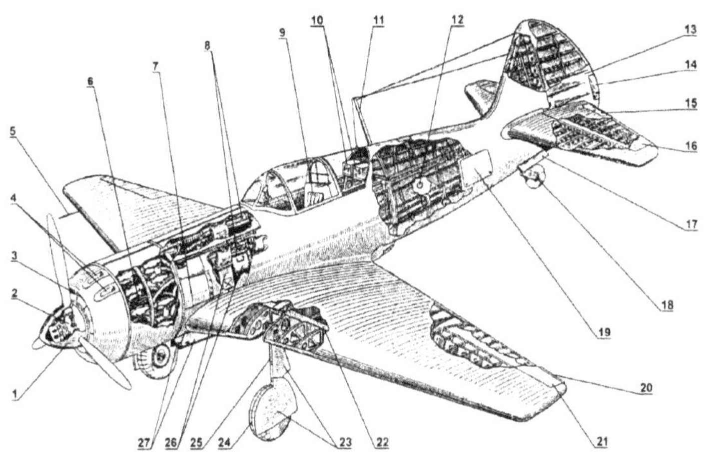

La-9 Layout:

1. Propeller hub
2. Propeller VISH-105V-4
3. Suction pipe
4. NS-23Z gun ports
5. Air pressure receiver
6. ASH-V2FN Engine
7. Engine cooling flap
8. NS-23 cannon
9. Pilot's seat
10. Radio equipment
11. Antenna mast
12. Pneumatic system door
13. Rudder
14. Rudder trimmer
15. Elevator trimmer
16. Tail plans
17. Cavity fins for cleaning the tip holder
18. Tail wheel
19. Fuselage

20. Aileron trimmers
21. Ailerons
22. Longheron
23. Main landing gear shields
24. Wheel
25. Trolley leg
26. Cartridge boxes
27. Guards covering the main landing gear wheel domes

Technical features

Dimensions and weights

- Length: 8.62 meters
- Wingspan: 9.80 meters
- Height: 2.69 meters
- Wing area: 17.60 m^2
- Wing loading: 195 km/m^2

Propulsion

- Engine: a Shvetsov Ash-82FN radial
- Power: 1,850 hp (1,361 kW)

Performance

- Maximum speed: 690 km/h
- Climb rate: 17.70 meters per second
- Autonomy: 1,735 km
- Tangency: 10,800 meters

Armament

- Guns: four Nudelman-Suranov NS-23 23 mm caliber

Nudelman-Suranov NS-23 cannon

The Nudelman-Suranov NS-23 was a 23 mm aircraft automatic cannon, designed in the Soviet Union as a replacement for the Volkov-Yartsev VYa-23.

The gun entered service in 1943, adopting the 14.5 × 114 mm anti-tank projectile and rechambering it in the 23 mm.

By 1943 the OKB-16 had developed a new 23 mm projectile, half as heavy as the VYa gun, for which a suitable gun was designed: ground tests were concluded in May 1944, and trials on the La-7 were also completed a month later.

- The NS-23 gun was 2 meters long, with a 1.45 meter barrel and weighed 37 kg, compared to 68 kg for the VYa gun.

It was operated by a short recoil, with counter-recoil by a coil spring and hydropneumatic cylinder.

It was produced in the NS-23KM variants for loyal and the engine and NS-23S with synchronized mechanism.

It fired 23x115 mm projectiles weighing 175-200 grams, with a rate of fire of 550 rounds per minute, as well as a muzzle velocity of 690 m/s.

- The barrel had a service life of 4,000 rounds.

It was produced from 1944 to 1953 in 58,479 units, of which 908 between 1944 and 1945.

The projectile consisted of a steel body with a sintered copper or iron guiding band and a tracer cavity in the rear.

It was filled with HE and capped at the top with a fake steel fuse cap.

A tracer self-destruct (SD) mechanism caused the projectile to explode when the tracer ran out.

The bullet was black in color and had white markings printed on it.
The dummy fuse's pin had a blue tip.

3 NS-23 cannons in the nose of the Lavochkin La-9.

The NR-23 was, basically, a modified variant of the NS-23, with the aim of increasing the rate of fire.
Engineer Richter was responsible for the mechanical "accelerator" introduced into this cannon.

- The accelerator is a part used in automatic cocking that increases the speed of movement of the bolt.

Of course, this increases the rate of fire which is around 750-800 rounds per minute.
The NR 23 fired the same cartridge as the NS 23 and was the armament used in the MiG-15, MiG 17, early MiG-19s and also as the defensive gun on the IL-28 and Antonov An-10.
The bomber emplacement has a steel reinforcement to reduce aerodynamic flutter.
Its barrel is slightly longer than the NS 23 and the recoil spring is covered by a cylindrical sheet metal.

www.ingramcontent.com/pod-product-compliance
Lightning Source LLC
LaVergne TN
LVHW010111170826
845678LV00012B/2354